TABLE OF CONTENTS

Top 20 Test Taking Tips

1. Carefully follow all the test registration procedures
2. Know the test directions, duration, topics, question types, how many questions
3. Setup a flexible study schedule at least 3-4 weeks before test day
4. Study during the time of day you are most alert, relaxed, and stress free
5. Maximize your learning style; visual learner use visual study aids, auditory learner use auditory study aids
6. Focus on your weakest knowledge base
7. Find a study partner to review with and help clarify questions
8. Practice, practice, practice
9. Get a good night's sleep; don't try to cram the night before the test
10. Eat a well balanced meal
11. Know the exact physical location of the testing site; drive the route to the site prior to test day
12. Bring a set of ear plugs; the testing center could be noisy
13. Wear comfortable, loose fitting, layered clothing to the testing center; prepare for it to be either cold or hot during the test
14. Bring at least 2 current forms of ID to the testing center
15. Arrive to the test early; be prepared to wait and be patient
16. Eliminate the obviously wrong answer choices, then guess the first remaining choice
17. Pace yourself; don't rush, but keep working and move on if you get stuck
18. Maintain a positive attitude even if the test is going poorly
19. Keep your first answer unless you are positive it is wrong
20. Check your work, don't make a careless mistake

POSS

Introduction

Congratulations! You have decided to take the Plant Operator Selection System (POSS) examination, which means you are pursuing employment as a power plant operator. This is an excellent career move, for a number of reasons. For many people, this kind of hands-on, active job is a perfect fit. Plant operators get to move around and work in a variety of different locations; they are never trapped behind a desk watching the hands of a clock! Plant operators perform a wide variety of tasks. They are required to work both independently and as part of a team. Also, because they have received specialized training, plant operators can be highly paid and receive excellent career benefits for their services.

Despite all of the physical and financial rewards of a career as a plant operator, many individuals find that meeting the mental challenges of the job is more satisfying. Plant operators are constantly required to solve problems both great and small. In order to keep a power plant functioning effectively, a huge number of calculations and adjustments are often made on a daily basis. For this reason, a plant operator needs to be adept at considering the various aspects of a problem and imagining realistic and viable solutions. Sometimes, the options available to the operator will be limited by resources. When this is the case, a plant operator has to be creative in improvising a solution. Despite outward appearances, therefore, the work of a plant operator is as much mental as physical.

Another great thing about being a plant operator is the variety of tasks required by the job. The specific duties of the plant operator will depend on the type of power plant in which one is working. For instance, the operator of an electrical power station must inspect equipment and keep detailed logs of performance and maintenance. He or she must manage the plant generators and solve problems with production as they arise. Moreover, a power plant operator must maintain safe working conditions for all of the members of his staff, and must demonstrate leadership during emergency situations. An operator at a water treatment plant, on the other hand, will have a slightly different set of duties. He or she may be required to monitor and repair filtration and treatment systems, or to supervise the maintenance of these systems. Water treatment plant operators may be required to collect and analyze water samples, and to make recommendations based on the test results.

As you can see, plant operators must be able to perform a wide range of tasks. All of these tasks, however, require the same basic skills. In order to succeed as a plant operator, you will need to be able to understand how objects are put together, read with understanding, make quick mechanical calculations, and solve basic math problems.

The Plant Operator Selection System (POSS) examination is designed to measure your knowledge and skill in these areas. This exam is primarily administered as part of the application process for employment by a municipality or private energy company. However, a high score on the POSS exam can also be a great way to bolster your resume as an independent contractor. Success on the POSS exam indicates that you have the knowledge and skills required to tackle a multitude of problems. Also, it indicates that you are serious about making a career in this field.

Unfortunately, many would-be plant operators miss out on a great career because they are intimidated by the idea of sitting for a written examination. Many people associate standardized tests with their time in school, and want to avoid the experience in any way possible. It is true that some of the topics covered on the POSS exam are similar to those found on more academic tests, like the SAT. However, the material on the POSS exam is specially adapted to be relevant to individuals interested in becoming a plant operator. Furthermore, in the assembly and mechanical concepts sections of the exam, the POSS exam focuses exclusively on problems that are likely to be encountered in the course of employment as a plant operator. Many test-takers find that they actually enjoy solving these problems; after all, it is this pleasure in solving mechanical problems that has led them to this line of work in the first place.

In any case, there is no reason why you should not succeed on the POSS exam. With the right kind of preparation, you can ensure a great score. This guidebook has been written as a comprehensive primer to the POSS exam. It contains detailed information about the content and types of questions you will encounter on examination day. After you have spent some time reading this book and practicing the kinds of exercises to be found on the exam, you should have no problem achieving an excellent score!

Test Format

The Plant Operator Selection System exam consists of five sections: assembly, mechanical concepts, tables and graphs, reading comprehension, and mathematical usage.

The assembly section tests your ability to mentally envision the form of an object after it has been properly assembled. This section of the exam consists of 20 multiple-choice questions, which must be completed within ten minutes. Each question is followed by five possible answers.

The mechanical concepts section measures your ability to comprehend the basic principles of mechanics. This section of the exam consists of 44 multiple-choice questions, which must be completed within 20 minutes. Each question is followed by three possible answers.

The tables and graphs section of the exam assesses your ability to obtain information from a table or graph quickly and accurately. This section of the exam is divided into two parts. In the first, you must answer 60 multiple-choice questions having to do with a table of numbers in five minutes. In the second part, you will be given four minutes to answer 24 multiple-choice questions having to do with a graph. In each part, the questions will be followed by four possible answers.

The reading comprehension section of the exam measures your ability to obtain information and make inferences based on expository texts. It consists of 32 multiple-choice questions, each with four possible answers. You must complete this section within thirty minutes.

Finally, the mathematical usage section assesses your ability to solve basic arithmetic problems. It consists of eighteen multiple-choice questions, each accompanied by five possible answers. You will have seven minutes in which to complete this portion of the exam.

In all, the POSS exam should take only a couple of hours to complete. You must complete the sections in the order in which they are given, and you will not be allowed to go back to a section once you have completed it. It is a good idea to bring your own pencil to the exam site, though extra pencils and scratch paper will be made available to those in need.

Scoring

You will be given five individual scores for each of the five sections of the exam. The five scores will be combined to produce an Index Score on a scale from 1 to 10. For all intents and purposes, this Index Score will be the record of your performance on the POSS exam. There is no minimum passing score recommended by the exam administrator; it will be up to your employer to judge your scores. Most scores fall between 3 and 8; both extremely low and extremely high scores are rare. Although the organization that produced the POSS does not make any official statement on the subject, former test administrators have let us know that there is a wrong answer penalty to discourage guessing. What this means for you is that unless you can eliminate two answer choices, guessing is probably not in your best interest.

On the day of the exam

When you register for the POSS exam, you will be given detailed information on where and when the examination will be given. The POSS exam is administered at testing facilities around the country; oftentimes, the exam will be administered by a large employer as part of the application process.

No matter where or when you take the exam, there are a few things you can do to maximize your performance. First, and perhaps most importantly, get a good night's sleep before your examination. You do not want to be groggy when you sit for the exam. Also, if you are taking the exam in the morning, be sure to eat a complete and balanced breakfast. Research consistently suggests that jumpstarting the body's metabolism with an early meal increases blood flow to the brain. Being hungry or weak from lack of food can inhibit your ability to concentrate during the exam. If you are taking the exam later in the day, bring a healthy snack (like a banana or a granola bar) to eat right before you begin. Also, be sure to drink plenty of water; like hunger, dehydration can make it difficult to focus your attention. Finally, be sure to wear clothes that are comfortable as well as appropriate for the testing environment. You want to make a good impression on the test administrator, but you also want to wear clothes that will not distract you while you work.

How to use this guide

This book endeavors to be a comprehensive guide to the Plant Operator Selection System (POSS) examination. It covers in detail all of the content and question types that will appear on your examination. It may be, however, that you are already fairly knowledgeable in one of the areas covered by the examination. If you are a math expert, for instance, you may already know much of the information covered in the mathematical usage section. For this reason, do not feel that you have to read this book from cover to cover. Feel free to concentrate your study on those areas of the examination for which you need the most preparation. If you have a limited time to study before the exam, focus your efforts on the content areas that are least familiar to you, as it is in these areas where you will see the most immediate improvement.

Moreover, you should not try to read this book in its entirety without interruption. A great deal of information has been condensed here, and it would be nearly impossible to retain all of it from a single reading. Here and there, we have indicated practice exercises that you can use to supplement the information contained in the book. Practicing the skills described herein is the best way to solidify your knowledge. Also, performing some practice exercises will accustom you to the type of thinking you'll have to do on the exam itself. The best way to use this book in preparation for the POSS exam is to read a little bit at a time for several weeks before the exam. If you can read and practice a small amount every day, you will steadily acquire all of the knowledge and skills you need to ace the exam!

Assembly

To begin with, let's take a look at the assembly section of the POSS exam. Many test-takers find that they feel most comfortable with this section of the exam because it plays to their natural strengths. Aspiring plant operators are likely to be people who enjoy taking things apart and putting them back together; working with their hands to get a sense of how machines are assembled. This section of the test measures your ability to imagine the way an object will look when its pieces are joined together properly. The 20 multiple-choice questions that make up this section will begin with a picture of five separate parts. Each of these parts will be marked with one or more letters. These letters will be assigned to places on the part. Sometimes the letter will appear directly over part of the object, and sometimes a line will be drawn from the letter to the appropriate spot on the object. If there is a dotted line drawn from the letter to the object, this means that the letter corresponds to a place on the side of the object that cannot be seen. Your task will be to imagine how the object will look when all of the parts are connected such that the letters touch one another. In other words, all of the parts marked with an *A* will need to touch; all of the parts marked with a *B* will need to touch, and so on. You will be given five assembled objects from which to choose your answer. This format will be the same for all twenty questions in the assembly section.

The format of the assembly questions, then, is fairly straightforward. However, you will only be given 10 minutes to solve these twenty problems, and therefore you will need to be able to work efficiently. This means approaching the assembly questions with a strategy in mind. There are a couple of different ways to proceed. Perhaps the best way to approach assembly questions is to proceed in order and work methodically. In other words, begin by mentally connecting the *A*s; once you have this assembly in mind, move on to the *B*s, and so forth. One mistake that many test-takers make is to attempt the entire assembly all at once. Many of these problems will involve four or five parts, and it will be too easy to get confused if you do not work in order. Indeed, the test administrator will be sure to include a few close-but-incorrect answers designed to trip up people who work too fast. The best way to proceed through an assembly question is to firmly decide on the arrangement of the object one piece at a time.

In tandem with this strategy, you can use the process of elimination to quickly reduce the number of possible answers. After you have mentally connected the *A*s, for instance, you can go through and rule out all of those answers that do not have the *A*s connected properly. You can then proceed through the Bs, ruling out a few more answers, until you are left with a single possible right answer, which you can then take a moment to confirm.

There are a few things to keep in mind when considering possible solutions to an assembly problem. To begin with, remember that the pieces can be turned in any way. They may be rotated, spun, and flipped. They may not, however, be folded, bent, or twisted. Furthermore, they may not change in size; each piece should be the same size in the answer as it is in the original picture. Occasionally, the makers of the POSS will place the pieces in the correct configuration but will drastically alter the sizes of one or more pieces. This automatically invalidates the answer. It is best to imagine the pieces as solid three-dimensional objects, which can be manipulated in all directions but cannot have their fundamental size and shape altered.

Similarly, make sure that the answer you select has the appropriate number of pieces. If there are five different components in the original drawing, there must be five connected parts in the answer. It is common for the exam to leave out a piece or include an extra piece in one or more of the possible answers; even if these answers are right in all other respects, they cannot be correct if they include more or fewer pieces than the original drawing.

Once you have worked through the problem in this systematic manner and have selected your answer, go back and double-check your work. To begin with, make sure that all of the letters are joined properly in the answer you have chosen. Then, make sure that your answer has the right number of pieces. Finally, make sure that the pieces in the assembled object are similar in size to the pieces in the original drawing. If all of these factors check out, you can be comfortable that you have selected the right answer.

This methodical way of working through assembly problems may seem too time-consuming given the limits of the exam, but with a little bit of practice you can speed through the process within the time given. In fact, by adhering to this organized way of solving assembly problems, you will actually save time, since you will never get confused or lost in a problem and have to go back to the beginning. All it takes to master these problems is a little strategic knowledge and a little preparation. Having covered the strategy, let's now take a look at a few ways to prepare for this section of the exam.

There are a few common activities you can use to prepare for the assembly section of the exam. For instance, even though jigsaw puzzles do not offer an exact replication of the items you will encounter on the POSS exam, they still exercise your spatial reasoning skills. Envisioning which pieces of the puzzle will fit together, and how the resulting arrangement will look, is a great way to hone your assembly skills. For an even greater challenge, try turning all the pieces of the puzzle face down, so that you cannot use the picture to guide your work: this will force you to rely more on your sense of orientation and arrangement.

Another way to prepare for this section of the exam is to take apart a small piece of machinery and study its configuration. Yard sales and junk bins are great places to find old appliances and electronics equipment. With the help of a screwdriver, wrench, and pair of pliers, you should be able to take apart most any appliance with ease. Once you have broken the item down into a pile of parts, see if you can put those parts back together into a functional whole. Even better, have someone else take apart the item and then see if you can put it back together. Of course, it is not recommended that you try this with valuable or expensive pieces of hardware. Also, some electronic appliances contain small batteries which should not be handled by non-professionals; always obey any warnings listed on the equipment. Nevertheless, taking apart and putting together small machines can be a fantastic way to improve your assembly skills.

Finally, there is a wealth of spatial intelligence exercises to be found on the Internet. Just by entering "spatial intelligence" into a search engine, you should receive listings for dozens of simple, free puzzles and games that strengthen your ability to visualize and perform basic assemblies. Some of these programs are so sophisticated that they allow you to manipulate three-dimensional objects on your computer screen! While for many people working on a computer is no substitute for direct contact with an object, these on-line exercises are a clean, fast way to stretch your mental muscles.

Whatever method you choose, be sure to prepare for at least a few hours before sitting for the POSS examination. For most students, the most difficult thing about the assembly questions is getting comfortable with the format and learning how to approach the problem. By remembering the strategies discussed above, and utilizing some of the suggested practice exercises, you can make sure that you will be ready to attack assembly problems immediately.

Mechanical Concepts

For most POSS test-takers, the mechanical concepts section of the exam is the most appealing. People who are interested in plant operation often have an intuitive sense of the physical world, the behavior of machines, and the best ways to accomplish a physical task. All of these areas are covered in the mechanical concepts questions. This section of the exam consists of 44 questions, and must be completed within 20 minutes. This may not seem like a great deal of time, but many of the questions will not require more than a few seconds of thought once you have solidified your understanding of the basic concepts of applied physics and mechanics. Each of the 44 questions will be based on a picture, and will have three possible answers. The pictures will contain all of the information required to answer the questions. Some of the questions have to do with specific simple machines, while others apply mechanics to more general topics.

In order to succeed on the mechanical concepts section of the POSS exam, you will need to be familiar with basic concepts in physics and mechanics. Don't worry: the POSS exam does not dwell on obscure theories or require you to make complicated calculations. The equations that are included in this section of the book are meant to illustrate the relationships of physics, not to show you how to solve numerical problems. You do, however, need to understand the essential properties of physics, and how they apply to real-life situations. In order to help you along, we have included a full primer on all of the concepts that may come up on this section of the exam. Important terms and concepts are placed in bold. Finally, although we have tried to make this section of the guidebook as easy to read as possible, we still recommend that you take your time and avoid reading in a hurry. You may need to read some of this information a few times before fully absorbing it. Whenever possible, try to imagine some everyday examples for the concepts we discuss; after all, applying the theories of physics to the materials of everyday life is one way to define mechanics.

Kinematics

To begin, we will look at the basics of physics. At its heart, physics is just a set of explanations for the ways in which matter and energy behave. There are three key concepts used to describe how matter moves:

1. Displacement
2. Velocity
3. Acceleration

Displacement

Concept: where and how far an object has gone
Calculation: final position – initial position

When something changes its location from one place to another, it is said to have undergone displacement. If a golf ball is hit across a sloped green into the hole, the displacement only takes into account the final and initial locations, not the path of the ball.

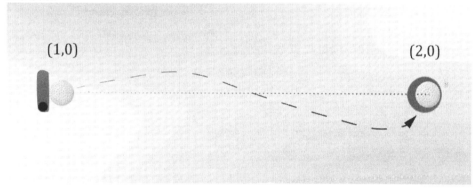

Displacement along a straight line is a very simple example of a vector quantity: that is, it has both a magnitude and a direction. Direction is as important as magnitude in many measurements. If we can determine the original and final position of the object, then we can determine the total displacement with this simple equation:

$$\text{Displacement} = \text{final position} - \text{original position}$$

The hole (final position) is at the Cartesian coordinate location (2, 0) and the ball is hit from the location (1, 0). The displacement is:

$$\text{Displacement} = (2,0) - (1,0)$$
$$\text{Displacement} = (1,0)$$

The displacement has a magnitude of 1 and a direction of the positive x direction.

> ➤ **Review Video: Displacement**
> *Visit* ***mometrix.com/academy*** *and enter* ***Code: 236197***

Velocity

Concept: the rate of moving from one position to another
Calculation: change in position / change in time

Velocity answers the question, "How quickly is an object moving?" For example, if a car and a plane travel between two cities which are a hundred miles apart, but the car takes two hours and the plane takes one hour, the car has the same displacement as the plane, but a smaller velocity.

In order to solve some of the problems on the exam, you may need to assess the velocity of an object. If we want to calculate the average velocity of an object, we must know two things. First, we must know its displacement. Second, we must know the time it took to cover this distance. The formula for average velocity is quite simple:

$$\textbf{average velocity} = \frac{\textbf{displacement}}{\textbf{change in time}}$$

Or

$$\textbf{average velocity} = \frac{\textbf{final position} - \textbf{original position}}{\textbf{final time} - \textbf{original time}}$$

To complete the example, the velocity of the plane is calculated to be:

$$\text{plane average velocity} = \frac{100 \text{ miles}}{1 \text{ hour}} = 100 \text{ miles per hour}$$

The velocity of the car is less:

$$\text{car average velocity} = \frac{100 \text{ miles}}{2 \text{ hours}} = 50 \text{ miles per hour}$$

Often, people confuse the words *speed* and *velocity*. There is a significant difference. The average velocity is based on the amount of displacement, a vector. Alternately, the average speed is based on the distance covered or the path length. The equation for speed is:

$$\text{average speed} = \frac{\text{total distance traveled}}{\text{change in time}}$$

Notice that we used total distance and *not* change in position, because speed is path-dependent.

If the plane traveling between cities had needed to fly around a storm on its way, making the distance traveled 50 miles greater than the distance the car traveled, the plane would still have the same total displacement as the car.

The calculation for the speed: For this reason, average speed can be calculated:

$$\text{plane average speed} = \frac{150 \text{ miles}}{1 \text{ hour}} = 150 \text{ miles per hour}$$

$$\text{car average speed} = \frac{100 \text{ miles}}{2 \text{ hours}} = 50 \text{ miles per hour}$$

> ➤ **Review Video:** <u>Speed and Velocity</u>
> *Visit **mometrix.com/academy** and enter **Code: 645590***

Acceleration

Concept: how quickly something changes from one velocity to another
Calculation: change in velocity / change in time

Acceleration is the rate of change of the velocity of an object. If a car accelerates from zero velocity to 60 miles per hour (88 feet per second) in two seconds, the car has an impressive acceleration. But if a car performs the same change in velocity in eight seconds, the acceleration is much lower and not as impressive.

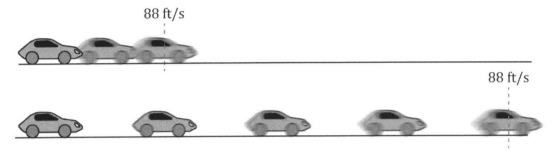

To calculate average acceleration, we may use the equation:

$$\text{average acceleration} = \frac{\text{change in velocity}}{\text{change in time}}$$

The acceleration of the cars is found to be:

$$\text{Car \#1 average acceleration} = \frac{88 \text{ feet per second}}{2 \text{ seconds}} = 44 \frac{\text{feet}}{\text{second}^2}$$

$$\text{Car \#2 average acceleration} = \frac{88 \text{ feet per second}}{8 \text{ seconds}} = 11 \frac{\text{feet}}{\text{second}^2}$$

Acceleration will be expressed in units of distance divided by time squared; for instance, meters per second squared or feet per second squared.

> ➤ **Review Video: <u>Velocity and Acceleration</u>**
> *Visit **mometrix.com/academy** and enter **Code: 311122***

Projectile Motion

A specific application of the study of motion is projectile motion. Simple projectile motion occurs when an object is in the air and experiencing only the force of gravity. We will disregard drag for this topic. Some common examples of projectile motion are thrown balls, flying bullets, and falling rocks. The characteristics of projectile motion are:

1. The horizontal component of velocity doesn't change
2. The vertical acceleration due to gravity affects the vertical component of velocity

Because gravity only acts downwards, objects in projectile motion only experience acceleration in the y direction (vertical). The horizontal component of the object's velocity does not change in flight. This means that if a rock is thrown out off a cliff, the horizontal velocity, (think the shadow if the sun is directly overhead) will not change until the ball hits the ground.

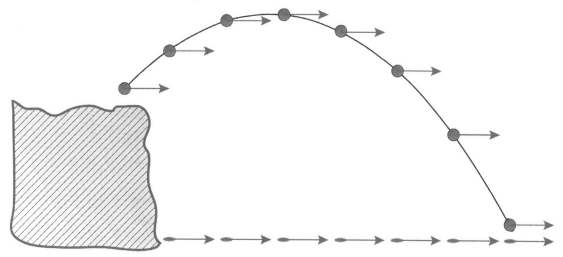

The velocity in the vertical direction is affected by gravity. Gravity imposes an acceleration of $g = 9.8 \frac{m}{s^2}$ or $32 \frac{ft}{s^2}$ downward on projectiles. The vertical component of velocity at any point is equal to:

vertical velocity = original vertical velocity − g × time

When these characteristics are combined, there are three points of particular interest in a projectile's flight. At the beginning of a flight, the object has a horizontal component and a vertical component giving it a large speed. At the top of a projectile's flight, the vertical velocity equals zero, making the top the slowest part of travel. When the object passes the same height as the launch, the vertical velocity is opposite of the initial vertical velocity making the speed equal to the initial speed.

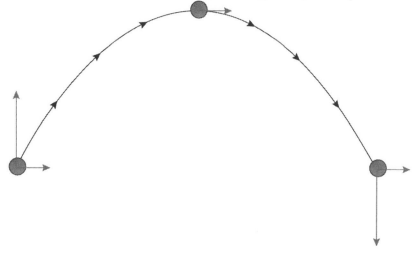

If the object continues falling below the initial height from which it was launched (e.g., it was launched from the edge of a cliff), it will have an even greater velocity than it did initially from that point until it hits the ground.

➢ **Review Video: Projectile Motion**
*Visit **mometrix.com/academy** and enter **Code: 719700***

Rotational Kinematics

Concept: increasing the radius increases the linear speed
Calculation: linear speed = radius × rotational speed

Another interesting application of the study of motion is rotation. In practice, simple rotation is when an object rotates around a point at a constant speed. Most questions covering rotational kinematics will provide the distance from a rotating object to the center of rotation (radius) and ask about the linear speed of the object. A point will have a greater linear speed when it is farther from the center of rotation.

If a potter is spinning his wheel at a constant speed of one revolution per second, the clay six inches away from the center will be going faster than the clay three inches from the center. The clay directly in the center of the wheel will not have any linear velocity.

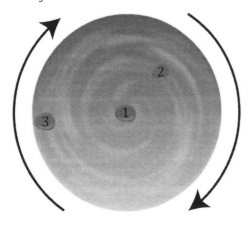

To find the linear speed of rotating objects using radians, we use the equation:

$$linear\ speed = (rotational\ speed\ [in\ radians]) \times (radius)$$

Using degrees, the equation is:

$$linear\ speed = (rotational\ speed\ [in\ degrees]) \times \frac{\pi\ radians}{180\ degrees} \times (radius)$$

To find the speed of the pieces of clay we use the known values (rotational speed of 1 revolution per second, radii of 0 inches, 3 inches, and 6 inches) and the knowledge that one revolution = 2 pi.

$$clay\ \#1\ speed = \left(2\pi \frac{rad}{s}\right) \times (0\ inches) = 0 \frac{inches}{second}$$

$$clay\ \#2\ speed = \left(2\pi \frac{rad}{s}\right) \times (3\ inches) = 18.8 \frac{inches}{second}$$

$$clay\ \#3\ speed = \left(2\pi \frac{rad}{s}\right) \times (6\ inches) = 37.7 \frac{inches}{second}$$

Kinetics

Newton's three laws of mechanics

The questions on the exam may require you to demonstrate familiarity with the concepts expressed in Newton's three laws of motion which relate to the concept of force.

Newton's first law – A body at rest will tend to remain at rest, while a body in motion will tend to remain in motion, unless acted upon by an external force.

Newton's second law – The acceleration of an object is directly proportional to the force being exerted on it and inversely proportional to its mass.

Newton's third law – For every force, there is an equal and opposite force.

First Law

Concept: Unless something interferes, an object won't start or stop moving

Although intuition supports the idea that objects do not start moving until a force acts on them, the idea of an object continuing forever without any forces can seem odd. Before Newton formulated his laws of mechanics, general thought held that some force had to act on an object continuously in order for it to move at a constant velocity. This seems to make sense: when an object is briefly pushed, it will eventually come to a stop. Newton, however, determined that unless some other force acted on the object (most notably friction or air resistance), it would continue in the direction it was pushed at the same velocity forever.

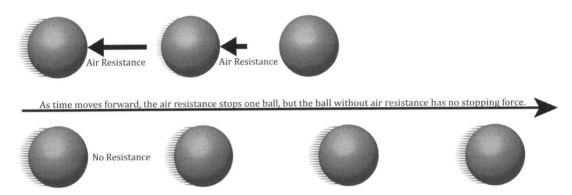

> ➤ **Review Video:** <u>Newton's First Law</u>
> *Visit **mometrix.com/academy** and enter **Code: 341140***

Second Law

Concept: Acceleration increases linearly with force.

Although Newton's second law can be conceptually understood as a series of relationships describing how an increase in one factor will decrease another factor, the law can be understood best in equation format:

$$Force = mass \times acceleration$$

Or

$$Acceleration = \frac{force}{mass}$$

Or

$$Mass = \frac{force}{acceleration}$$

Each of the forms of the equation allows for a different look at the same relationships. To examine the relationships, change one factor and observe the result. If a steel ball, with a diameter of 6.3 cm, has a mass of 1 kg and an acceleration of 1 m/s², then the net force on the ball will be 1 Newton.

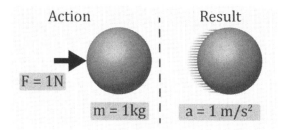

➢ **Review Video: Newton's Second Law**
*Visit **mometrix.com/academy** and enter **Code: 324555***

Third Law

Concept: Nothing can push or pull without being pushed or pulled in return.

When any object exerts a force on another object, the other object exerts the opposite force back on the original object. To observe this, consider two spring-based fruit scales, both tipped on their sides as shown with the weighing surfaces facing each other. If fruit scale #1 is pressing fruit scale #2 into the wall, it exerts a force on fruit scale #2, measurable by the reading on scale #2. However, because fruit scale #1 is exerting a force on scale #2, scale #2 is exerting a force on scale #1 with an opposite direction, but the same magnitude.

➢ **Review Video: Newton's Third Law**
*Visit **mometrix.com/academy** and enter **Code: 909605***

Force

Concept: a push or pull on an object
Calculation: $Force = mass \times acceleration$

A force is a vector which causes acceleration of a body. Force has both magnitude and direction. Furthermore, multiple forces acting on one object combine in vector addition. This can be demonstrated by considering an object placed at the origin of the coordinate plane. If it is pushed along the positive direction of the x-axis, it will move in this direction; if the force acting on it is in the positive direction of the y-axis, it will move in that direction.

However, if both forces are applied at the same time, then the object will move at an angle to both the x and y axes, an angle determined by the relative amount of force exerted in each direction. In this way, we may see that the resulting force is a vector sum; that is, a net force that has both magnitude and direction.

Resultant vectors from applied forces:

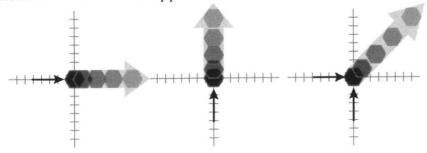

> ➤ **Review Video: Force**
> *Visit **mometrix.com/academy** and enter **Code: 104731***

Mass

Concept: the amount of matter

Mass can be defined as the quantity of matter in an object. If we apply the same force to two objects of different mass, we will find that the resulting acceleration is different. Newton's Second Law of Motion describes the relationship between mass, force, and acceleration in the equation: ***Force = mass x acceleration***. In other words, the acceleration of an object is directly proportional to the force being exerted on it and inversely proportional to its mass.

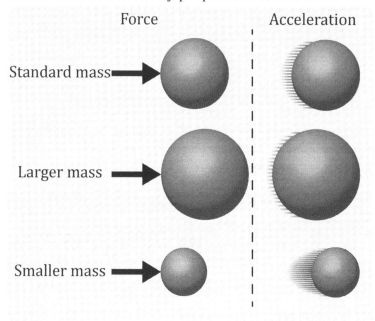

Gravity

Gravity is a force which exists between all objects with matter. Gravity is a pulling force between objects meaning that the forces on the objects point toward the opposite object. When Newton's third law is applied to gravity, the force pairs from gravity are shown to be equal in magnitude and opposite in direction.

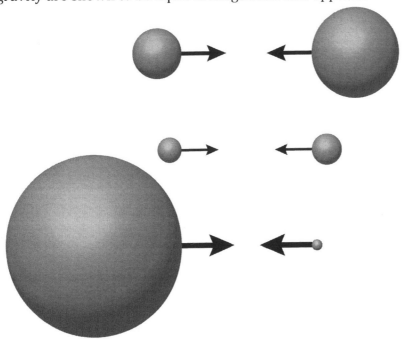

Weight

Weight is sometimes confused with mass. While mass is the amount of matter, weight is the force exerted by the earth on an object with matter by gravity. The earth pulls every object of mass toward its center while every object of mass pulls the earth toward its center. The object's pull on the earth is equal in magnitude to the pull which the earth exerts, but, because the mass of the earth is very large in comparison (5.97×10^{24} kg), only the object appears to be affected by the force.

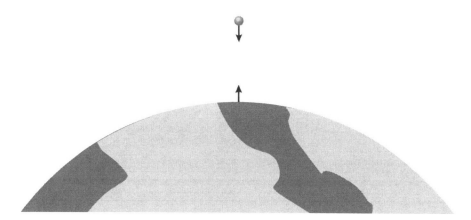

The gravity of earth causes a constant acceleration due to gravity (g) at a specific altitude. For most earthbound applications the acceleration due to gravity is 32.2 ft/s² or 9.8 m/s² in a downward direction. The equation for the force of gravity (weight) on an object is the equation from Newton's Second Law with the constant acceleration due to gravity (g).

$$Force = mass \times acceleration$$
$$Weight = mass \times acceleration \ due \ to \ gravity$$
$$W = m \times g$$

The SI (International Standard of Units) unit for weight is the Newton $\left(\frac{kg \times m}{s^2}\right)$. The English Engineering unit system uses the pound, or lb, as the unit for weight and force $\left(\frac{slug \times ft}{s^2}\right)$. Thus, a 2 kg object under the influence of gravity would have a weight of:

$$W = m \times g$$
$$W = 2 \text{ kg} \times 9.8 \frac{m}{s^2} = 18.6 \text{ N downwards}$$

> ➤ **Review Video: Mass and Weight**
> *Visit **mometrix.com/academy** and enter **Code: 104567***

Normal force

Concept: the force perpendicular to a contact surface

The word "normal" is used in mathematics to mean perpendicular, and so the force known as normal force should be remembered as the perpendicular force exerted on an object that is resting on some other surface. For instance, if a box is resting on a horizontal surface, we may say that the normal force is directed upwards through the box (the opposite, downward force is the weight of the box). If the box is resting on a wedge, the normal force from the wedge is not vertical but is perpendicular to the wedge edge.

 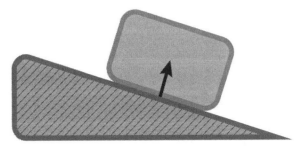

Tension

Concept: the pulling force from a cord

Another force that may come into play on the exam is called tension. Anytime a cord is attached to a body and pulled so that it is taut, we may say that the cord is under tension. The cord in tension applies a pulling tension force on the connected objects. This force is pointed away from the body and along the cord at the point of attachment. In simple considerations of tension, the cord is assumed to be both without mass and incapable of stretching. In other words, its only role is as the connector between two bodies. The cord is also assumed to pull on both ends with the same magnitude of tension force.

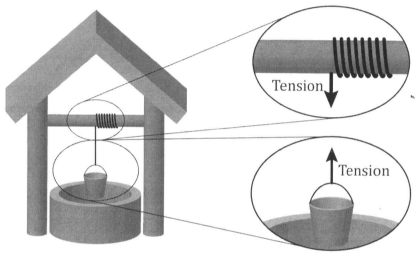

Friction

Concept: Friction is a resistance to motion between contacting surfaces

In order to illustrate the concept of friction, let us imagine a book resting on a table. As it sits, the force of its weight is equal to and opposite of the normal force. If, however, we were to exert a force on the book, attempting to push it to one side, a frictional force would arise, equal and opposite to our force. This kind of frictional force is known as static frictional force.

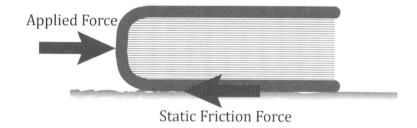

- 29 -

As we increase our force on the book, however, we will eventually cause it to accelerate in the direction of our force. At this point, the frictional force opposing us will be known as kinetic friction. For many combinations of surfaces, the magnitude of the kinetic frictional force is lower than that of the static frictional force, and consequently, the amount of force needed to maintain the movement of the book will be less than that needed to initiate the movement.

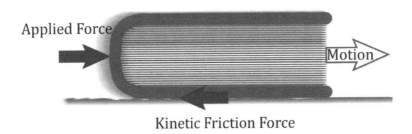

> **Review Video:** <u>Friction</u>
> *Visit **mometrix.com/academy** and enter **Code:** 264932*

Rolling Friction

Occasionally, a question will ask you to consider the amount of friction generated by an object that is rolling. If a wheel is rolling at a constant speed, then the point at which it touches the ground will not slide, and there will be no friction between the ground and the wheel inhibiting movement. In fact, the friction at the point of contact between the wheel and the ground is static friction necessary to propulsion with wheels. When a vehicle accelerates, the static friction between the wheels and ground allows the vehicle to achieve acceleration. Without this friction, the vehicle would spin its wheels and go nowhere.

Although the static friction does not impede movement for the wheels, a combination of frictional forces can resist rolling motion. One such frictional force is bearing friction. Bearing friction is the kinetic friction between the wheel and an object it rotates around, such as a stationary axle.

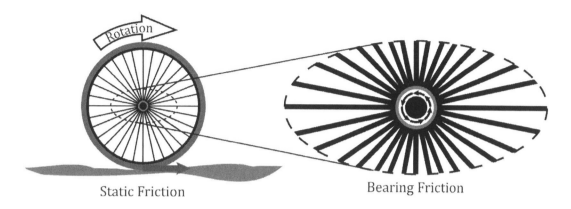

Static Friction   Bearing Friction

Drag force

Friction can also be generated when an object is moving through air or liquid. A drag force occurs when a body moves through some fluid (either liquid or gas) and experiences a force that opposes the motion of the body. The drag force is greater if the air or fluid is thicker or is moving in the direction opposite to the object. Obviously, the higher the drag force, the greater amount of positive force required to keep the object moving forward.

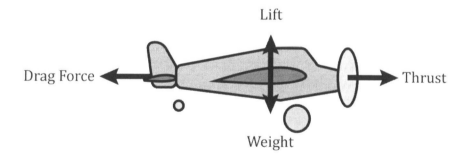

Lift

Drag Force ←→ Thrust

Weight

Balanced Forces

An object is in equilibrium when the sum of all forces acting on the object is zero. When the forces on an object sum to zero, the object does not accelerate. Equilibrium can be obtained when forces in the y-direction sum to zero, forces in the x-direction sum to zero, or forces in both directions sum to zero.

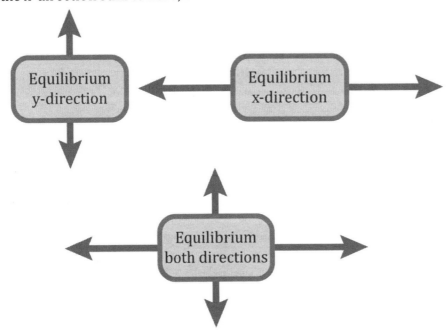

In most cases, a problem will provide one or more forces acting on object and ask for a force to balance the system. The force will be the opposite of the current force or sum of current forces.

Balance the forces

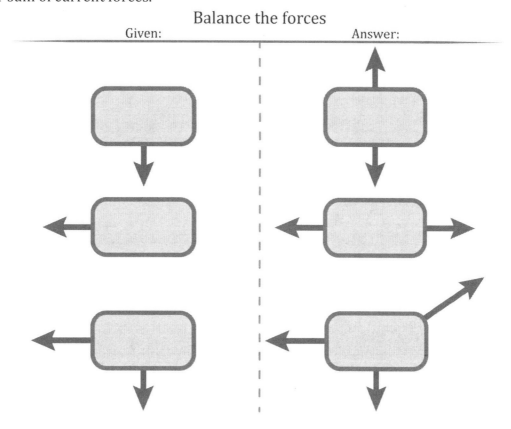

Rotational Kinetics

Many equations and concepts in linear kinematics and kinetics transfer to rotation. For example, angular position is an angle. Angular velocity, like linear velocity, is the change in the position (angle) divided by the time. Angular acceleration is the change in angular velocity divided by time. Although most tests will not require you to perform angular calculations, they will expect you to understand the angular version of force: torque.

Concept: Torque is a twisting force on an object
Calculation: $Torque = radius \times force$

Torque, like force, is a vector and has magnitude and direction. As with force, the sum of torques on an object will affect the angular acceleration of that object. The key to solving problems with torque is understanding the lever arm. A better description of the torque equation is:

Torque
= force × the distance perpedicular to the force to the center of rotation

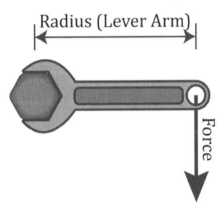

Because torque is directly proportional to the radius, or lever arm, a greater lever arm will result in a greater torque with the same amount of force. The wrench on the right has twice the radius and, as a result, twice the torque.

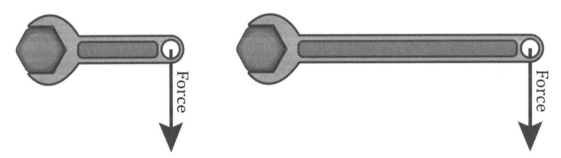

Alternatively, a greater force also increases torque. The wrench on the right has twice the force and twice the torque.

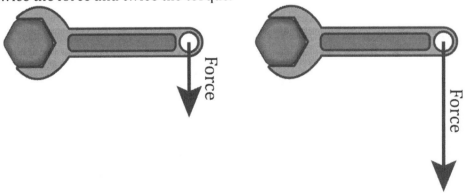

Work/Energy

Work

Concept: Work is the transfer of energy from one object to another
Calculation: Work = force × displacement

The equation for work in one dimension is fairly simple:
$$Work = Force \times displacement$$
$$W = F \times d$$

In the equation, the force and the displacement are the magnitude of the force exerted and the total change in position of the object on which the force is exerted, respectively. If force and displacement have the same direction, then the work is positive. If they are in opposite directions, however, the work is negative.

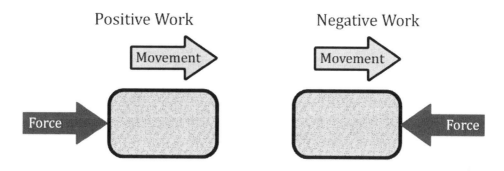

> ➤ **Review Video:** Work
> *Visit **mometrix.com/academy** and enter **Code: 257801***

Energy

Concept: the ability of a body to do work on another object

Energy is a word that has found a million different uses in the English language, but in physics it refers to the measure of a body's ability to do work. In physics, energy may not have a million meanings, but it does have many forms. Each of these forms, such as chemical, electric, and nuclear, is the capability of an object to perform work. However, for the purpose of most tests, mechanical energy and mechanical work are the only forms of energy worth understanding in depth. Mechanical energy is the sum of an object's kinetic and potential energies. Although they will be introduced in greater detail, these are the forms of mechanical energy:

Kinetic Energy – energy an object has by virtue of its motion
Gravitational Potential Energy – energy by virtue of an object's height
Elastic Potential Energy – energy stored in compression or tension

Neglecting frictional forces, mechanical energy is conserved.

As an example, imagine a ball moving perpendicular to the surface of the earth, with its weight the only force acting on it. As the ball rises, the weight will be doing work on the ball, decreasing its speed and its kinetic energy, and slowing it down until it momentarily stops. During this ascent, the potential energy of the ball will be rising. Once the ball begins to fall back down, it will lose potential energy as it gains kinetic energy. Mechanical energy is conserved throughout; the potential energy of the ball at its highest point is equal to the kinetic energy of the ball at its lowest point prior to impact.

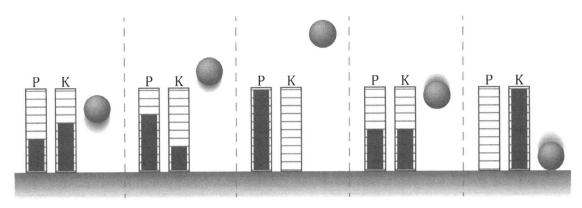

In systems where friction and air resistance are not negligible, we observe a different sort of result. For example, imagine a block sliding across the floor until it comes to a stop due to friction. Unlike a compressed spring or a ball flung into the air, there is no way for this block to regain its energy with a return trip. Therefore, we cannot say that the lost kinetic energy is being stored as potential energy. Instead, it has been dissipated and cannot be recovered. The total mechanical energy of the block-floor system has been not conserved in this case but rather reduced. The total energy of the system has not decreased, since the kinetic energy has been converted into thermal energy, but that energy is no longer useful for work.

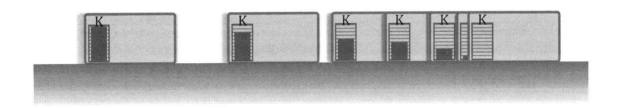

Energy, though it may change form, will be neither created nor destroyed during physical processes. However, if we construct a system and some external force performs work on it, the result may be slightly different. If the work is positive, then the overall store of energy is increased; if it is negative, however, we can say that the overall energy of the system has decreased.

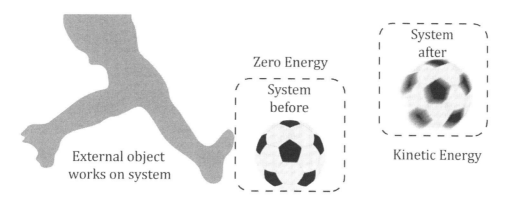

➢ **Review Video:** <u>Energy</u>
*Visit **mometrix.com/academy** and enter **Code: 677735***

Kinetic energy

The kinetic energy of an object is the amount of energy it possesses by reason of being in motion. Kinetic energy cannot be negative. Changes in kinetic energy will occur when a force does work on an object, such that the motion of the object is altered. This change in kinetic energy is equal to the amount of work that is done. This relationship is commonly referred to as the work-energy theorem.

One interesting application of the work-energy theorem is that of objects in a free fall. To begin with, let us assert that the force acting on such an object is its weight, equal to its mass times *g* (the force of gravity). The work done by this force will be positive, as the force is exerted in the direction in which the object is traveling. Kinetic energy will, therefore, increase, according to the work-kinetic energy theorem.

If the object is dropped from a great enough height, it eventually reaches its terminal velocity, where the drag force is equal to the weight, so the object is no longer accelerating and its kinetic energy remains constant.

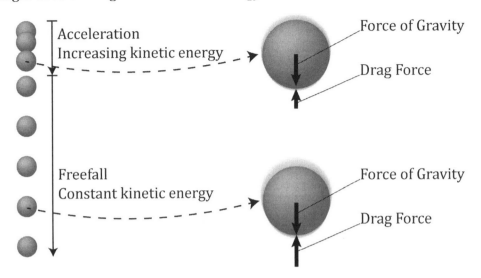

Gravitational Potential Energy

Gravitational potential energy is simply the potential for a certain amount of work to be done by one object on another using gravity. For objects on earth, the gravitational potential energy is equal to the amount of work which the earth can act on the object. The work which gravity performs on objects moving entirely or partially in the vertical direction is equal to the force exerted by the earth (weight) times the distance traveled in the direction of the force (height above the ground or reference point):

Work from gravity = weight × height above the ground

Thus, the gravitational potential energy is the same as the potential work.

Gravitational Potential Energy = weight × height

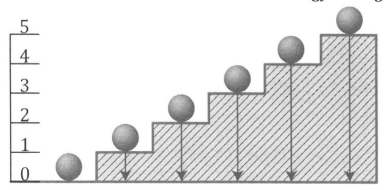

> ➤ **Review Video:** <u>Potential and Kinetic Energy</u>
> *Visit **mometrix.com/academy** and enter **Code:** 173339*

Elastic Potential Energy

Elastic potential energy is the potential for a certain amount of work to be done by one object on another using elastic compression or tension. The most common example is the spring. A spring will resist any compression or tension away from its equilibrium position (natural position). A small buggy is pressed into a large spring. The spring contains a large amount of elastic potential energy. If the buggy and spring are released, the spring will push exert a force on the buggy for a distance. This work will put kinetic energy into the buggy. The energy can be imagined as a liquid poured from one container into another. The spring pours its elastic energy into the buggy, which receives the energy as kinetic energy.

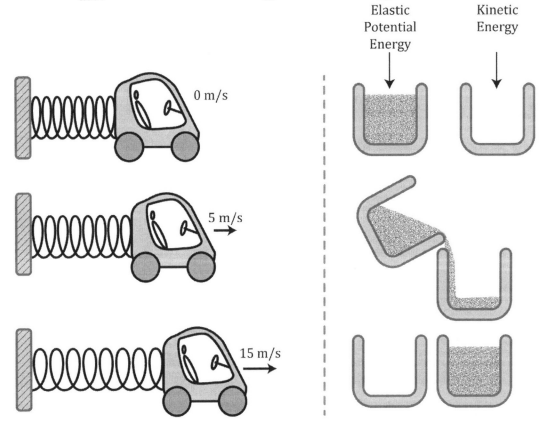

Power

Concept: the rate of work
Calculation: work/time

On occasion, you may need to demonstrate an understanding of power, as it is defined in applied physics. Power is the rate at which work is done. Power, like work and energy, is a scalar quantity. Power can be calculated by dividing the amount of work performed by the amount of time in which the work was performed.

$$\textbf{Power} = \frac{\textbf{work}}{\textbf{time}}$$

If more work is performed in a shorter amount of time, more power has been exerted. Power can be expressed in a variety of units. The preferred metric expression is one of watts or joules per seconds. For engine power, it is often expressed in horsepower.

Machines

Simple machines

Concept: Tools which transform forces to make tasks easier.

As their job is to transform forces, simple machines have an input force and an output force or forces. Simple machines transform forces in two ways: direction and magnitude. A machine can change the direction of a force, with respect to the input force, like a single stationary pulley which only changes the direction of the output force. A machine can also change the magnitude of the force like a lever.

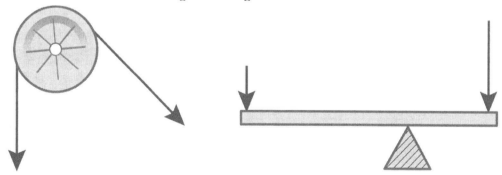

Simple machines include the inclined plane, the wedge, the screw, the pulley, the lever, and the wheel.

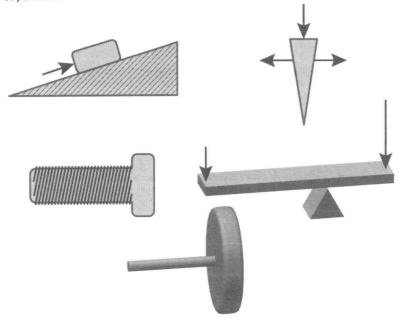

Mechanical Advantage

Concept: the amount of change a simple machine provides to the magnitude of a force
Calculation: output force/input force

Mechanical advantage is the measure of the output force divided by the input force. Thus, mechanical advantage measures the change performed by a machine. Machines cannot create energy, only transform it. Thus, in frictionless, ideal machines, the input work equals the output work.

$$Work_{input} = Work_{output}$$
$$force_{input} \times distance_{input} = force_{output} \times distance_{output}$$

This means that a simple machine can increase the force of the output by decreasing the distance which the output travels or it can increase the distance of the output by decreasing the force at the output.

By moving parts of the equation for work, we can arrive at the equation for mechanical advantage.

$$\textbf{Mechanical Advantage} = \frac{\textbf{force}_{\textbf{output}}}{\textbf{force}_{\textbf{input}}} = \frac{\textbf{distance}_{\textbf{input}}}{\textbf{distance}_{\textbf{output}}}$$

If the mechanical advantage is greater than one, the output force is greater than the input force and the input distance is greater than the output distance. Conversely, if the mechanical advantage is less than one, the input force is greater than the output force and the output distance is greater than the input distance. In equation form this is:

If Mechanical Advantage > 1:
$$force_{input} < force_{output} \text{ and } distance_{output} < distance_{input}$$

If Mechanical Advantage < 1:
$$force_{input} > force_{output} \text{ and } distance_{output} > distance_{input}$$

Inclined plane

The inclined plane is perhaps the most common of the simple machines. It is simply a flat surface that elevates as you move from one end to the other; a ramp is an easy example of an inclined plane. Consider how much easier it is for an elderly person to walk up a long ramp than to climb a shorter but steeper flight of stairs; this is because the force required is diminished as the distance increases. Indeed, the longer the ramp, the easier it is to ascend.

On the exam, this simple fact will most often be applied to moving heavy objects. For instance, if you have to move a heavy box onto the back of a truck, it is much easier to push it up a ramp than to lift it directly onto the truck bed. The longer the ramp, the greater the mechanical advantage, and the easier it will be to move the box. The mechanical advantage of an inclined plane is equal to the slant length divided by the rise of the plane.

$$\text{Mechanical Advantage} = \frac{\text{slant length}}{\text{rise}}$$

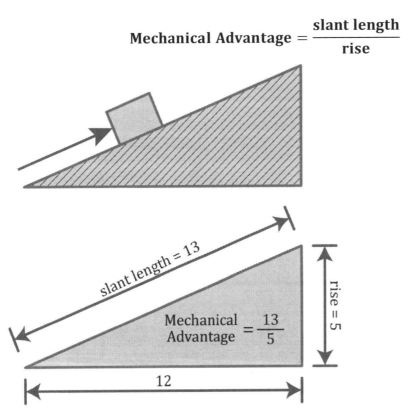

As you solve this kind of problem, however, remember that the same amount of work is being performed whether the box is lifted directly or pushed up a twenty-foot ramp; a simple machine only changes the force and the distance.

Wedge

A wedge is a variation on the inclined plane, in which the wedge moves between objects or parts and forces them apart. The unique characteristic of a wedge is that, unlike an inclined plane, it is designed to move. Perhaps the most familiar use of the wedge is in splitting wood. A wedge is driven into the wood by hitting the flat back end. The thin end of a wedge is easier to drive into the wood since it has less surface area and, therefore, transmits more force per area. As the wedge is driven in, the increased width helps to split the wood.

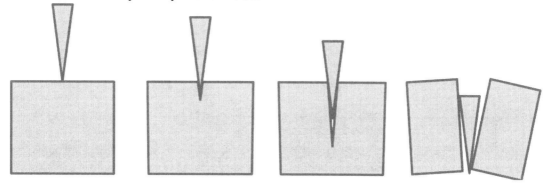

The exam may require you to select the wedge that has the highest mechanical advantage. This should be easy: the longer and thinner the wedge, the greater the mechanical advantage. The equation for mechanical advantage is:

$$\textbf{Mechanical Advantage} = \frac{\textbf{Length}}{\textbf{Width}}$$

> ➤ **Review Video:** <u>Wedge and Inclined Plane</u>
> *Visit* ***mometrix.com/academy*** *and enter* ***Code: 103334***

Screw

A screw is simply an inclined plane that has been wound around a cylinder so that it forms a sort of spiral.

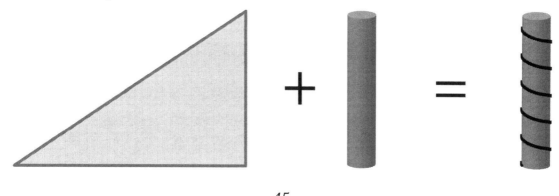

When it is placed into some medium, as for instance wood, the screw will move either forward or backward when it is rotated. The principle of the screw is used in a number of different objects, from jar lids to flashlights. On the exam, you are unlikely to see many questions regarding screws, though you may be presented with a given screw rotation and asked in which direction the screw will move. However, for consistency's sake, the equation for the mechanical advantage is a modification of the inclined plane's equation. Again, the formula for an inclined plane is:

$$Mechanical\ Advantage = \frac{slant\ length}{rise}$$

Because the rise of the inclined plane is the length along a screw, length between rotations = rise. Also, the slant length will equal the circumference of one rotation = $2\pi r$.

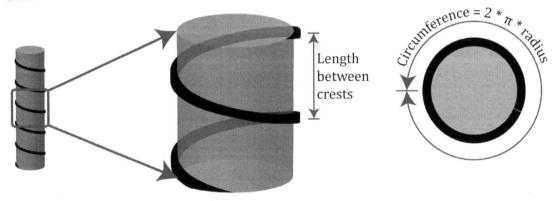

$$\mathbf{Mechanical\ Advantage} = \frac{\mathbf{2 \times \pi \times radius}}{\mathbf{length\ between\ crests}}$$

Lever

The lever is the most common kind of simple machine. See-saws, shovels, and baseball bats are all examples of levers. There are three classes of levers which are differentiated by the relative orientations of the fulcrum, resistance, and effort. The fulcrum is the point at which the lever rotates; the effort is the point on the lever where force is applied; the resistance is the part of the lever that acts in response to the effort.

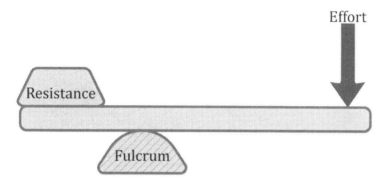

The mechanical advantage of a lever depends on the distances of the effort and resistance from the fulcrum. Mechanical advantage equals:

$$\textbf{Mechanical Advantage} = \frac{\textbf{effort distance}}{\textbf{resistance distance}}$$

For each class of lever, the location of the important distances changes:

First Class Lever

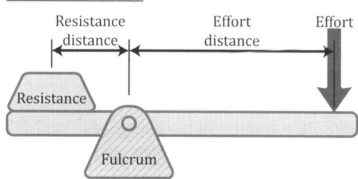

Second Class Lever

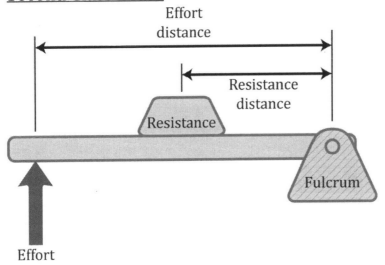

Third Class Lever

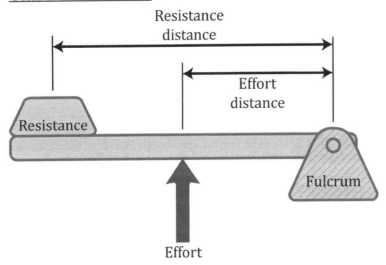

In a first class lever, the fulcrum is between the effort and the resistance. A seesaw is a good example of a first class lever: when effort is applied to force one end up, the other end goes down, and vice versa. The shorter the distance between the fulcrum and the resistance, the easier it will be to move the resistance. As an example, consider whether it is easier to lift another person on a see-saw when they are sitting close to the middle or all the way at the end. A little practice will show you that it is much more difficult to lift a person the farther away he or she is on the see-saw.

In a second class lever, the resistance is in-between the fulcrum and the effort. While a first class lever is able to increase force and distance through mechanical advantage, a second class lever is only able to increase force. A common example of a second class lever is the wheelbarrow: the force exerted by your hand at one end of the wheelbarrow is magnified at the load. Basically, with a second class lever you are trading distance for force; by moving your end of the wheelbarrow a bit farther, you produce greater force at the load.

Third class levers are used to produce greater distance. In a third class lever, the force is applied in between the fulcrum and the resistance. A baseball bat is a classic example of a third class lever; the bottom of the bat, below where you grip it, is considered the fulcrum. The end of the bat, where the ball is struck, is the resistance. By exerting effort at the base of the bat, close to the fulcrum, you are able to make the end of the bat fly quickly through the air. The closer your hands are to the base of the bat, the faster you will be able to make the other end of the bat travel.

> ➤ **Review Video:** Levers
> *Visit* **mometrix.com/academy** *and enter* **Code: 268220**

Pulley

The pulley is a simple machine in which a rope is carried by the rotation of a wheel. Another name for a pulley is a block. Pulleys are typically used to allow the force to be directed from a convenient location. For instance, imagine you are given the task of lifting a heavy and tall bookcase. Rather than tying a rope to the bookcase and trying to lift it up, it would make sense to tie a pulley system to a rafter above the bookcase and run the rope through it, so that you could pull down on the rope and lift the bookcase. Pulling down allows you to incorporate your weight (normal force) into the act of lifting, thereby making it easier.

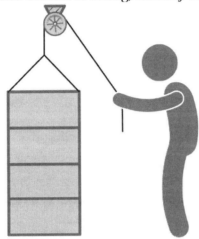

This item is on loan from an

OhioLINK
Institution

OVERDUE FINES:

- 50¢/day
- 30 days or more= $50
- Lost/damaged=$125

*FINES ARE NON-NEGOTIABLE
PER OHIOLINK GUIDELINES*

HOW TO RENEW:

- Online:
  www.loraincc.edu/library
  click "My Library Account"
  under Quick Links
- On the Phone:
  (440) 366-4026
- In Person:
  Bass Library 2nd floor
  Circulation Desk

QUESTIONS/HELP:

- Interlibrary Loan office:
  (440) 366-7336
- Email: ill@loraincc.edu

Items can be renewed up
to *six* times if no holds
have been placed on them.

Library
-HOURS-

FALL & SPRING SEMESTERS:

Mon-Thur.	8:00am-9:00pm
Friday	8:00am-4:30pm
Saturday	10:00am-3:00pm
Sunday	12:00pm-4:00pm

Please check our website
for hours between semesters

LIBRARY PHONE NUMBERS

(440) 366-4026 **(Circulation)**

(440) 366-4106 **(Research)**

(440)366-7336 **(Interlibrary Loan)**

Renewal Due Date:

1. _____

2. _____

3. _____

4. _____

5. _____

6. _____

Lorain County Community College

If there is just one pulley above the bookcase, you have created a first-class lever which will not diminish the amount of force that needs to be applied to lift the bookcase. There is another way to use a pulley, however, that can make the job of lifting a heavy object considerably easier. First, tie the rope directly to the rafter. Then, attach a pulley to the top of the bookcase and run the rope through it. If you can then stand so that you are above the bookcase, you will have a much easier time lifting this heavy object. Why? Because the weight of the bookcase is now being distributed: half of it is acting on the rafter, and half of it is acting on you. In other words, this arrangement allows you to lift an object with half the force. This simple pulley system, therefore, has a mechanical advantage of 2. Note that in this arrangement, the unfixed pulley is acting like a second-class lever. The price you pay for your mechanical advantage is that whatever distance you raise your end of the rope, the bookcase will only be lifted half as much.

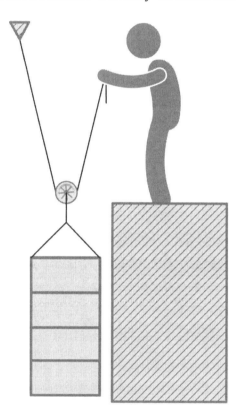

Of course, it might be difficult for you to find a place high enough to enact this system. If this is the case, you can always tie another pulley to the rafter and run the rope through it and back down to the floor. Since this second pulley is fixed, the mechanical advantage will remain the same.

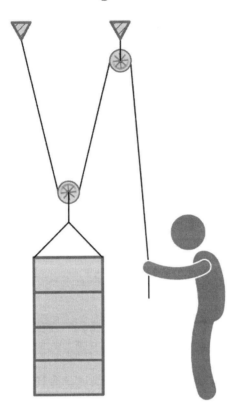

There are other, slightly more complex ways to obtain an even greater mechanical advantage with a system of pulleys. On the exam, you may be required to determine the pulley and tackle (rope) arrangement that creates the greatest mechanical advantage. The easiest way to determine the answer is to count the number of ropes that are going to and from the unfixed pulley; the more ropes coming and going, the greater the mechanical advantage.

> ➤ **Review Video: Pulley**
> Visit ***mometrix.com/academy*** *and enter* ***Code: 939636***

Wheel and axle

Another basic arrangement that makes use of simple machines is called the wheel and axle. When most people think of a wheel and axle, they immediately envision an automobile tire. The steering wheel of the car, however, operates on the same mechanical principle, namely that the force required to move the center of a circle is much greater than the force require to move the outer rim of a circle. When you turn the steering wheel, you are essentially using a second-class lever by increasing the output force by increasing the input distance. The force required to turn the wheel from the outer rim is much less than would be required to turn the wheel from its center. Just imagine how difficult it would be to drive a car if the steering wheel was the size of a saucer!

Conceptually, the mechanical advantage of a wheel is easy to understand. For instance, all other things being equal, the mechanical advantage created by a system will increase along with the radius. In other words, a steering wheel with a radius of 12 inches has a greater mechanical advantage than a steering wheel with a radius of ten inches; the same amount of force exerted on the rim of each wheel will produce greater force at the axis of the larger wheel.

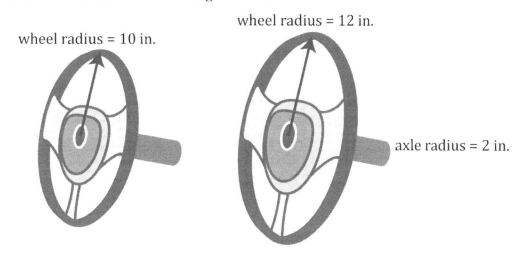

The equation for the mechanical advantage of a wheel and axle is:
$$\textbf{Mechanical Advantage} = \frac{\textbf{radius}_{\textbf{wheel}}}{\textbf{radius}_{\textbf{axle}}}$$

Thus, the mechanical advantage of the steering wheel with a larger radius will be:
$$Mechanical\ Advantage = \frac{12\ inches}{2\ inches} = 6$$

➢ **Review Video: Wheel and Axle**
Visit ***mometrix.com/academy*** *and enter* ***Code:*** **825035**

Gears

The exam may ask you questions involving some slightly more complex mechanisms. It is very common, for instance, for there to be a couple of questions concerning gears. Gears are a system of interlocking wheels that can create immense mechanical advantages. The amount of mechanical advantage, however, will depend on the gear ratio; that is, on the relation in size between the gears.

When a small gear is driving a big gear, the speed of the big gear is relatively slow; when a big gear is driving a small gear, the speed of the small gear is relatively fast.

The equation for the mechanical advantage is:

$$\textbf{Mechanical Advantage} = \frac{\textbf{Torque}_{\textbf{output}}}{\textbf{Torque}_{\textbf{input}}} = \frac{r_{\textbf{output}}}{r_{\textbf{input}}} = \frac{\textbf{\# of teeth}_{\textbf{output}}}{\textbf{\# of teeth}_{\textbf{input}}}$$

Note that mechanical advantage is greater than 1 when the output gear is larger. In these cases, the output velocity (ω) will be lower. The equation for the relative speed of a gear system is:

$$\frac{\omega_{\textbf{input}}}{\omega_{\textbf{output}}} = \frac{r_{\textbf{output}}}{r_{\textbf{input}}}$$

$$Mechanical\ Advantage = \frac{teeth_{output}}{teeth_{input}} = \frac{20}{10} = 2$$

$$Mechanical\ Advantage = \frac{teeth_{output}}{teeth_{input}} = \frac{16}{8} = 2$$

Uses of Gears

Gears are used to change direction of output torque, change location of output torque, change amount of output torque, and change angular velocity of output.

Change output direction

Change torque location

Change torque amount

Change output velocity

Gear Ratios

A gear ratio is a measure of how much the speed and torque are changing in a gear system. It is the ratio of output speed to input speed. Because the number of teeth is directly proportional to the speed in meshing gears, a gear ratio can also be calculated using the number of teeth on the gears. When the driving gear has 30 teeth and the driven gear has 10 teeth, the gear ratio is 3:1.

$$Gear\ Ratio = \frac{\#\ of\ teeth_{driving}}{\#\ of\ teeth_{driven}} = \frac{30}{10} = \frac{3}{1} = 3:1$$

This means that the smaller, driven gear rotates 3 times for every 1 rotation of the driving gear.

➢ **Review Video:** Gears
*Visit **mometrix.com/academy** and enter **Code: 103100***

The Hydraulic Jack

The hydraulic jack is a simple machine using two tanks and two pistons to change the amount of an output force.

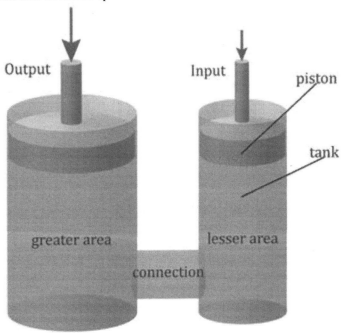

Since fluids are effectively incompressible, when you apply pressure to one part of a contained fluid, that pressure will have to be relieved in equal measure elsewhere in the container. Supposed the input piston has half the surface area of the output piston (10 in² compared to 20 in²), and it is being pushed downward with 50 pounds of force. The pressure being applied to the fluid is $50\ lb \div 10\ in^2 = 5\frac{lb}{in^2}$ or 5 psi. When that 5 psi of pressure is applied to the output piston, it pushes that piston upward with a force of $5\frac{lb}{in^2} \times 20\ in^2 = 100\ lb.$

The hydraulic jack functions similarly to a first class lever, but with the important factor being the area of the pistons rather than the length of the lever arms. Note that the mechanical advantage is based on the relative areas, not the relative radii, of the pistons. The radii must be squared to compute the relative areas.

$$\textbf{Mechanical Advantage} = \frac{\textbf{Force}_{\textbf{output}}}{\textbf{Force}_{\textbf{input}}} = \frac{\textbf{area}_{\textbf{output}}}{\textbf{area}_{\textbf{input}}} = \frac{\textbf{radius}_{\textbf{output}}^{2}}{\textbf{radius}_{\textbf{input}}^{2}}$$

Pulleys and Belts

Another system involves two pulleys connected by a drive belt (a looped band that goes around both pulleys). The operation of this system is similar to that of gears, with the exception that the pulleys will rotate in the same direction, while interlocking gears will rotate in opposite directions. A smaller pulley will always spin faster than a larger pulley, though the larger pulley will generate more torque.

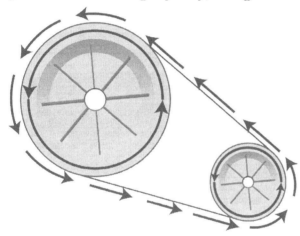

The speed ratio between the pulleys can be determined by comparing their radii; for instance, a 4-inch pulley and a 12-inch pulley will have a speed ratio of 3:1.

Momentum/Impulse

Linear momentum

Concept: how much a body will resist stopping
Calculation: *momentum = mass × velocity*

In physics, linear momentum can be found by multiplying the mass and velocity of an object:

$$\textbf{Momentum} = \textbf{mass} \times \textbf{velocity}$$

- 57 -

Momentum and velocity will always be in the same direction. Newton's second law describes momentum, stating that the rate of change of momentum is proportional to the force exerted and is in the direction of the force. If we assume a closed and isolated system (one in which no objects leave or enter, and upon which the sum of external forces is zero), then we can assume that the momentum of the system will neither increase nor decrease. That is, we will find that the momentum is a constant. The law of conservation of linear momentum applies universally in physics, even in situations of extremely high velocity or with subatomic particles.

Collisions

This concept of momentum takes on new importance when we consider collisions. A collision is an isolated event in which a strong force acts between each of two or more colliding bodies for a brief period of time. However, a collision is more intuitively defined as one or more objects hitting each other.

When two bodies collide, each object exerts a force on the opposite member. These equal and opposite forces change the linear momentum of the objects. However, when both bodies are considered, the net momentum in collisions is conserved.

There are two types of collisions: elastic and inelastic. The difference between the two lies in whether kinetic energy is conserved. If the total kinetic energy of the system is conserved, the collision is elastic. Visually, elastic collisions are collisions in which objects bounce perfectly. If some of the kinetic energy is transformed into heat or another form of energy, the collision is inelastic. Visually, inelastic collisions are collisions in which the objects do not bounce perfectly or even stick to each other.

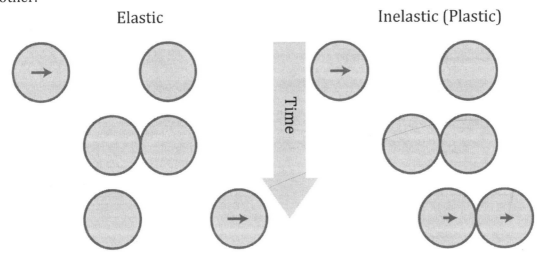

- 58 -

If the two bodies involved in an elastic collision have the same mass, then the body that was moving will stop completely, and the body that was at rest will begin moving at the same velocity as the projectile was moving before the collision.

Fluids

Fluids

Concept: liquids and gasses

A few of the questions on the exam will probably require you to consider the behavior of fluids. It sounds obvious, perhaps, but fluids can best be defined as substances that flow. A fluid will conform, slowly or quickly, to any container in which it is placed. Both liquids and gasses are considered to be fluids. Fluids are essentially those substances in which the atoms are not arranged in any permanent, rigid way. In ice, for instance, atoms are all lined up in what is known as a crystalline lattice, while in water and steam the only intermolecular arrangements are haphazard connections between neighboring molecules.

Flow Rates

When liquids flow in and out of containers with certain rates, the change in volume is the volumetric flow in minus the volumetric flow out. Volumetric flow is essentially the amount of volume moved past some point divided by the time it took for the volume to pass.

$$\textbf{Volumetric flow rate} = \frac{\textbf{volume moved}}{\textbf{time for the movement}}$$

If the flow into a container is greater than the flow out, the container will fill with the fluid. However, if the flow out of a container is greater than the flow into a container, the container will drain of the fluid.

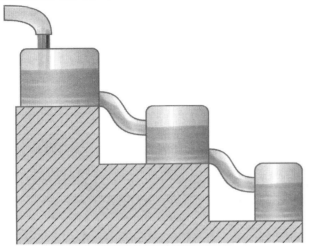

➢ **Review Video: Liquid and Hydraulics**
Visit mometrix.com/academy and enter Code: **103422**

Density

Concept: how much mass is in a specific volume of a substance
Calculation: $density = \rho = \frac{mass}{volume}$

Density is essentially how much stuff there is in a volume or space. The density of a fluid is generally expressed with the symbol ρ (the Greek letter rho.) The density may be found with the simple equation:

$$density = \rho = \frac{mass}{volume}$$

Density is a scalar property, meaning that it has no direction component.

➢ **Review Video: Density**
Visit mometrix.com/academy and enter Code: **104567**

Pressure

Concept: The amount of force applied per area

Calculation: $Pressure = \frac{force}{area}$

Pressure, like fluid density, is a scalar and does not have a direction. The equation for pressure is concerned only with the magnitude of that force, not with the direction in which it is pointing. The SI unit of pressure is the Newton per square meter, or Pascal.

$$\textbf{Pressure} = \frac{\textbf{force}}{\textbf{area}}$$

As every deep-sea diver knows, the pressure of water becomes greater the deeper you go below the surface; conversely, experienced mountain climbers know that air pressure decreases as they gain a higher altitude. These pressures are typically referred to as hydrostatic pressures because they involve fluids at rest.

Pascal's principle

The exam may also require you to demonstrate some knowledge of how fluids move. Anytime you squeeze a tube of toothpaste, you are demonstrating the idea known as Pascal's principle. This principle states that a change in the pressure applied to an enclosed fluid is transmitted undiminished to every portion of the fluid as well as to the walls of the containing vessel.

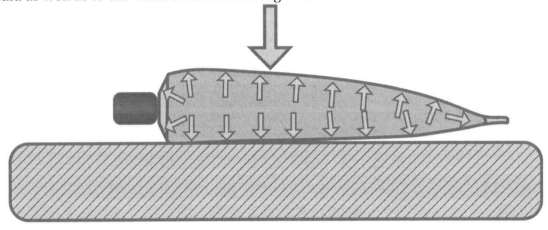

> ➤ **Review Video: Pressure**
> *Visit **mometrix.com/academy** and enter **Code: 995054**

Buoyant force

If an object is submerged in water, it will have a buoyant force exerted on it in the upward direction. Often, of course, this buoyant force is much too small to keep an object from sinking to the bottom. Buoyancy is summarized in Archimedes' principle; a body wholly or partially submerged in a fluid will be buoyed up by a force equal to the weight of the fluid that the body displaces.

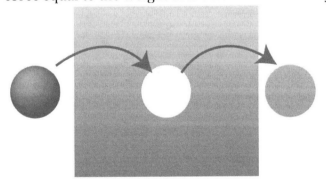

If the buoyant force is greater than the weight of an object, the object will go upward. If the weight of the object is greater than the buoyant force, the object will sink. When an object is floating on the surface, the buoyant force has the same magnitude as the weight.

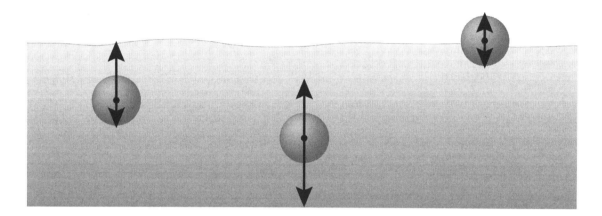

Bernoulli's principle

When fluids move, they do not create or destroy energy; this modification of Newton's second law for fluid behavior is called Bernoulli's principle. It is essentially just a reformulation of the law of conservation of mechanical energy for fluid mechanics.

The most common application of Bernoulli's principle is that pressure and speed are inversely related, assuming constant altitude. Thus if the elevation of the fluid remains constant and the speed of a fluid particle increases as it travels along a streamline, the pressure will decrease. If the fluid slows down, the pressure will increase.

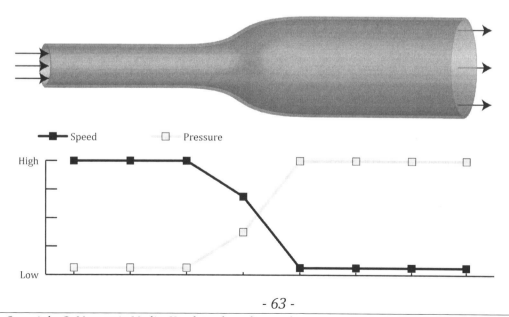

Heat Transfer

Heat is a type of energy. Heat transfers from the hot object to the cold object through the three forms of heat transfer: conduction, convection, and radiation.

| Conduction | Convection | Radiation |

Conduction is the transfer of heat by physical contact. When you touch a hot pot, the pot transfers heat to your hand by conduction.

Convection is the transfer of heat by the movement of fluids. When you put your hand in steam, the steam transfers heat to your hand by convection.

Radiation is the transfer of heat by electromagnetic waves. When you put your hand near a campfire, the fire heats your hand by radiation.

> ➤ **Review Video:** <u>Heat Transfer</u>
> *Visit **mometrix.com/academy** and enter **Code:** 451646*

Phase Changes

Materials exist in four phases or states: solid, liquid, gas, and plasma. However, as most tests will not cover plasma, we will focus on solids, liquids, and gases. The solid state is the densest in almost all cases (water is the most notable exception), followed by liquid, and then gas.

Solid   Liquid   Gas

The impetus for phase change (changing from one phase to another) is heat. When a solid is heated, it will change into a liquid. The same process of heating will change a liquid into a gas.

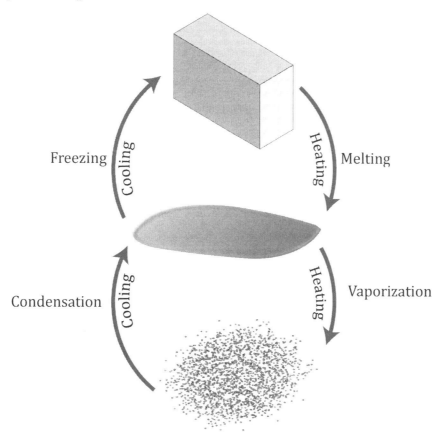

Freezing   Cooling   Heating   Melting

Condensation   Cooling   Heating   Vaporization

Electricity

Electric Charge

Much like gravity, electricity is an everyday observable phenomenon which is very complex, but may be understood as a set of behaviors. As the gravitational force exists between objects with mass, the electric force exists between objects with electrical charge. In all atoms, the protons have a positive charge, while the electrons have a negative charge. An imbalance of electrons and protons in an object results in a net charge. Unlike gravity, which only pulls, electrical forces can push objects apart as well as pulling them together.

Similar electric charges repel each other. Opposite charges attract each other.

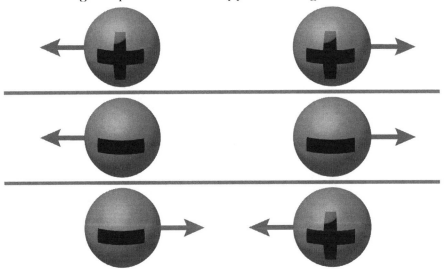

> ➤ **Review Video:** Electric Charge
> *Visit **mometrix.com/academy** and enter **Code:** 115908*

Current

Electrons (and electrical charge with it) move through conductive materials by switching quickly from one atom to another. This electrical flow can manipulate energy like mechanical systems.

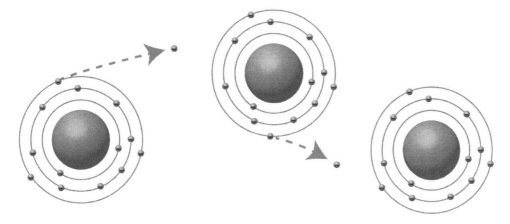

The term for the rate at which the charge flows through a conductive material is current. Because each electron carries a specific charge, current can be thought of as the number of electrons passing a point in a length of time. Current is measured in Amperes (A), each unit of which is approximately 6.24×10^{18} electrons per second.

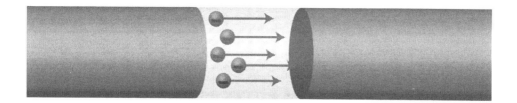

Electric current carries energy much like moving balls carry energy.

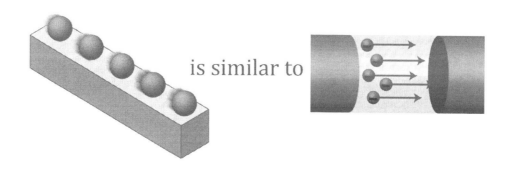

is similar to

Voltage

Voltage is the potential for electric work. Voltage is the push behind electrical work. Voltage is similar to gravitational potential energy.

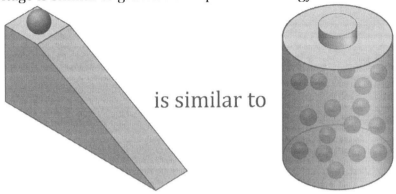

is similar to

Anything used to generate a voltage, such as a battery or a generator, is called a voltage source. Voltage is conveniently measured in Volts (V).

Resistance

Resistance is the amount of pressure to slow electrical current. Electrical resistance is much like friction, resisting flow and dissipating energy.

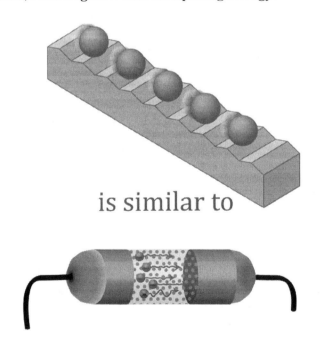

is similar to

Different objects have different resistances. A resistor is an electrical component designed to have a specific resistance, measured in Ohms (Ω).

Basic Circuits

A circuit is a closed loop through which current can flow. A simple circuit contains a voltage source and a resistor. The current flows from the positive side of the voltage source through the resistor to the negative side of the voltage source.

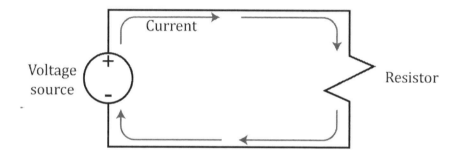

If we plot the voltage of a simple circuit, the similarities to gravitational potential energy appear.

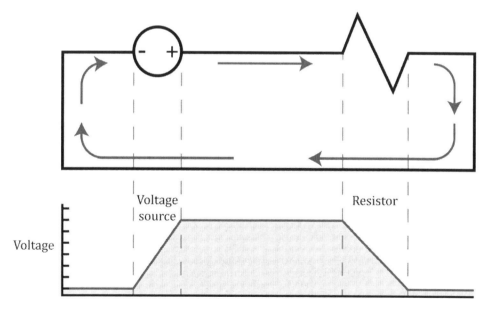

If we consider the circuit to be a track, the electrons would be balls, the voltage source would be a powered lift, and the resistor would be a sticky section of the track. The lift raises the balls, increasing their potential energy. This potential energy is expended as the balls roll down the sticky section of the track.

Voltage Source

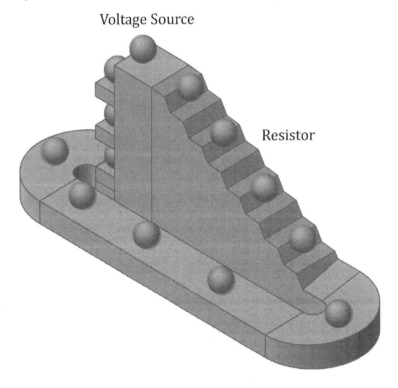

Resistor

> **Review Video: Circuits**
*Visit **mometrix.com/academy** and enter **Code: 388595***

Magnetism

Magnetism is an attraction between opposite poles of magnetic materials and a repulsion between similar poles of magnetic materials. Magnetism can be natural or induced with the use of electric currents. Magnets almost always exist with two polar sides: north and south. A magnetic force exists between two poles on objects. Different poles attract each other. Like poles repel each other.

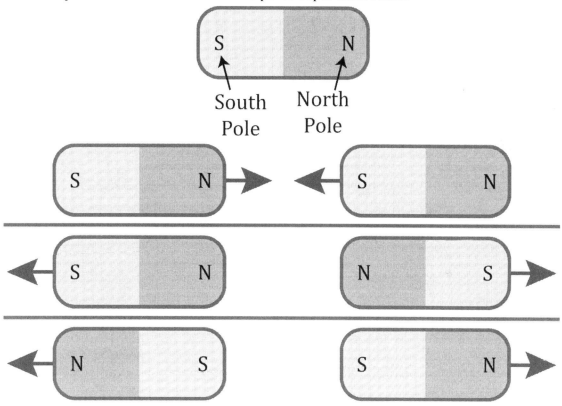

> ➤ **Review Video:** [Magnets](#)
> *Visit **mometrix.com/academy** and enter **Code: 993343***

Tables and Graphs

The tables and graphs section of the POSS exam is a test of skill and speed. In this section, you are required to use information from tables and graphs to answer a series of straightforward questions. The professional life of a plant operator requires constant creation and interpretation of charts and tables. Indeed, these formats for organizing and presenting information are invaluable tools for a plant operator; it is only through tables and charts that we are able to discern patterns in large sets of data. In order to perform your job knowledgably, then, you will need to be fluent in the use of tables and charts.

> ➢ **Review Video: Graphs**
> Visit *mometrix.com/academy* and enter *Code:* **355505**

The tables and graphs section of the POSS exam is divided into two parts. In the first part, you will be shown a detailed table of data and asked to answer 60 multiple-choice questions within five minutes. In the second part, you will be given a graph and asked to answer 24 multiple-choice questions within four minutes. In both parts of the tables and graphs section, questions will be accompanied by four or five possible answers.

To begin with, then, let's consider the tables you are likely to encounter on the POSS exam. By definition, tables are a way of presenting a set of data in a structured, organized format. A great deal of information can be placed into a relatively small area through the use of a table. In order to get the maximum value from a table, however, you need to be able to read it correctly. If you have used a basic computer database or spreadsheet program, then you will be familiar with the types of tables that appear on the POSS exam. They are grids composed of vertical and horizontal lines, and these lines form small blocks, known as cells, in which individual values are placed.

There is a simple and systematic way to approach a data table. When you are presented with a table, your first step should be to read the title and subheadings. The title will appear atop the table, and will define the data contained in the body of the table. As an example, look at the table below, which describes the distance covered by a series of projectiles with different masses fired at different angles to the ground:

Distance (in meters)

Mass	Angle 15 degrees	25 degrees	45 degrees	60 degrees	75 degrees
10 grams	32.662	37.890	43.773	42.643	32.736
20 grams	35.267	39.769	46.472	44.927	35.197
30 grams	37.883	43.794	51.906	49.268	39.331
40 grams	36.212	43.642	54.788	52.712	41.282
50 grams	36.021	42.022	49.764	47.881	40.899
60 grams	33.908	40.086	45.782	43.659	36.173

The title of this table is **Distance (in meters)**, as this is what the numerical data on the interior of the table represents. Note that because the units are given in the title of the table, it is not necessary to include them in the table itself. The table also includes two subheadings: **Mass** and **Angle**. The subheadings define the values that extend along the left and top borders of the table, respectively. The units used for each subheading maybe given in the subheading or may simply be appended to the numerical amounts, as in this table. Along the left border, then, we have the masses of the various projectiles, given in order from least to greatest. Along the top border, we have the angles at which the various projectiles were fired, also proceeding from least to greatest. When values are arranged with a specific order, as they are here, they are known as ordinals. Please remember that values are not always placed in an order; they may simply be given at random. When the values along the border are placed without a specific order, they are referred to as nominals.

In order to determine the distance traveled by a projectile with a given mass fired at a given angle, we will simply move across the appropriate mass row until we come to the appropriate angle column (in a table, horizontal groups are called rows and vertical groups are called columns). This is the simple structure of every question in the first part of the tables and graphs section. Let us take a look at an example:

Mass	Angle	A	B	C	D
30 g	45°	49.268	51.906	46.472	43.794

This is the exact question format you will see on the POSS exam. You are given the mass and angle values, and asked to determine the distance as it is listed in the table. To do so, simply find the row for 30 grams and move to the right until you find the value beneath 45 degrees. If you find that it helps you to use your scratch paper to isolate the 30 gram column, by all means do so. You can also trace across with your finger or pencil to make sure that you stay in the right row and column. Whatever method you use, you should find that the 30-gram projectile fired at an angle of 45 degrees traveled 51.906 meters.

Here is another sample question:

Mass	Angle	A	B	C	D
40 g	60 °	41.282	47.881	52.712	43.659

Beginning in the 40 gram row, trace across until you reach the 60 degree row. In other words, the cell you are looking for is in both the 40 gram row and the 60 degree column. The answer to this problem is 52.712 meters. If you can, try to find the answer in the table before looking at the answer choices. This will keep you from being influenced by the presence of nearby cells among the answer choices. If you find what you believe to be the right answer on your own and then see that it is among the available answer choices, you can be doubly sure that you have found the right answer.

The first part of the tables and graphs section, then, is fairly straightforward. The above example questions exactly mimic the types of questions that you will see on the exam. The most important thing to remember when working through these problems is to proceed deliberately and calmly, and to double-check your work after you select an answer. Once you have practiced a bit, you will be able to extract information from a table with plenty of time to spare.

In the second part of the exam, you will be presented with a simple graph. The line graph is the format most commonly used in this section of the exam. Line graphs represent data along two axes, known as the *x* and *y* (horizontal and vertical, respectively) axes. As with a table, the most important first step to accurately interpreting a graph is to read the title and subheadings. Take a look at the graph below:

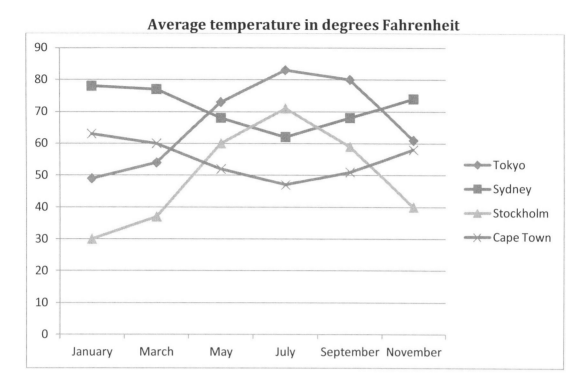

Average temperature in degrees Fahrenheit

The title of the graph is **Average temperature in degrees Fahrenheit**. Along the vertical axis, you will see numbers representing the various average temperatures. Along the horizontal axis, you will see the names of the months, from January to November. Notice that the months proceed in order, but that one month is skipped in between. In other words, we must assume that February lies in between January and March, April lies between March and May, etc. Within the body of the graph, four lines represent four different cities: Tokyo (blue line marked with diamond); Sydney (red line marked with square); Stockholm (green line marked with triangle); and Cape Town (purple line marked with cross). The placement of the markings on each line corresponds with a month listed on the horizontal axis; the farthest left mark, for instance, corresponds to January.

Once you know how to read a graph, you should find that obtaining information from it is as easy as obtaining information from a table. The only complication when dealing with a graph is that you will not always be dealing with exact numerical values.

As an example, take a look at the following example question:

Temperature	Month	A	B	C	D
78°	March	Tokyo	Sydney	Stockholm	Cape Town

This question wants you to determine which of the four cities has an average temperature of 78 degrees during the month of March. Of course, the graph does not contain exact temperature data, so you will be required to examine it to determine which city most likely fits the description. If you look at the map, you will notice that only one city has an average temperature between 70 and 80 degrees during the month of March: Sydney. Furthermore, the line for Sydney is rather closer to 80 degrees than to 70 degrees, so it is quite reasonable to assume that the average temperature in Sydney in March is 78 degrees. The answer, then, will be B.

As you can see, this question is not much more difficult than those from part one. Occasionally, though, the test administrator will require you to do a bit more thinking to obtain the right answer. For instance, you might see a problem like the following:

Temperature	Month	A	B	C	D
51°	October	Tokyo	Sydney	Stockholm	Cape Town

Immediately, you should note that the month of October is not specifically listed on the horizontal axis of the graph. You know, of course, that October comes between September and November, and therefore you may assume it to be denoted by the notch in between these months on the horizontal axis. Proceeding up from this notch, then, we see that the green line for Stockholm and the purple line for Cape Town are both in between 50 and 60 degrees in October. However, the line for Stockholm is much closer to the 50 degree line, and therefore appears much more to be representing 51 degrees. The purple line for Cape Town would seem to be closer to 54 degrees. As you can see, a minimal amount of deductive reasoning is required to interpret these graphs. With a little practice, though, this kind of problem should not give you any trouble at all.

The graph problems in part two of the tables and graph section do not get any more complicated than this. For most students, the hardest thing about the tables and graphs section of the POSS exam is answering all of the questions within the time limit. Given enough time, the vast majority of test-takers would be able to answer every question correctly with ease. However, under the time constraints imposed by the exam administrator, many people rush their work and make careless mistakes. For this reason, you should establish good habits and work as quickly as possible.

In order to make sure you are ready for the tables and graphs section of the exam, you should spend a little time practicing these skills before the exam date. Luckily, it is not hard at all to find examples of tables and graphs. Inside any encyclopedia or almanac (not to mention the World Wide Web), there are scores of tables and graphs you can use for practice. You can make up your own practice questions or have a friend ask you questions based on the information in the table or graph. At first, concentrate on answering every question correctly; once you have achieved perfect accuracy, you can focus on increasing your speed. With a couple of hours of practice in advance of the exam, you should be more than ready to ace the tables and graphs section of the POSS!

Reading Comprehension

Every POSS examination will contain a section of reading comprehension questions. Although critical reading skills are not normally considered to be part of the repertoire of a plant operator, in actuality you will be required to read and understand a number of different texts during the course of your service. For one thing, you will often have to engage in written correspondence with your employer or with your fellow employees. You need to be able to understand written directions and descriptions of equipment and operations. You will also have to stay abreast of the latest techniques and products used in the field, and for this you will need to be able to read and understand catalogs and training manuals. Finally, you may need to read local, state, and national regulations in order to avoid violating the law. The area in which you work may be heavily regulated by the government, and so it is no exaggeration to say that your livelihood and the livelihood of your employer may depend on your ability to understand that which you read.

With this in mind, let's take a look at the reading comprehension questions that will appear on the POSS exam. As mentioned above, the reading comprehension section will include 32 multiple-choice questions that must be completed within 30 minutes. These questions will be based on four passages of several paragraphs each. These passages will pertain to topics related to energy, power plants, and other subjects related to the field of plant operation. However, you will not be required to have any special knowledge to answer the reading comprehension questions. In fact, the directions in this section will specifically warn you to base your answers solely on the information found within the passage; in other words, do not base your answers on your own experience or knowledge of a particular subject.

It is important, then, to remember the purpose of the reading comprehension questions is to test your reading ability, and not to assess your knowledge of the topic. The reading comprehension exercises on the exam are designed to assess your ability to read carefully, analyze the relationships among different parts of a passage, and draw inferences from the material in the passage. The reading comprehension questions on the exam are of four basic types (main idea, detail, tone, and extending the author's reasoning), each of which calls for a slightly different approach.

The format of reading comprehension questions should not pose any problems. Each of the four passages will be followed by eight questions. These questions will be in a multiple-choice format, with four or five possible correct answers. For the most part, questions pertaining to the beginning of the passage will come before questions pertaining to the end of the passage. The reading comprehension questions on the exam are meant to be comprehensible to a general audience, and will not contain any specialized jargon. The passages should be as comprehensible to newcomers as they are to experts. Now, let's take a quick look at the content of the passages that will appear on the exam.

The reading comprehension passages on POSS exams all pertain to subjects related to plant operation, though they may come from a number of different genres. At least one of the passages will be an excerpt from a training manual of some kind. This passage will feature clear, technical language and a strict attention to organization. Training manuals outline the steps in a process and tend to proceed in a clear and orderly fashion. Other passages will be written in a legal style, and will pertain to operational regulations or building codes. These passages will be dense and full of information; you are likely to be asked to recall specific details. When you are confronted with an extremely technical passage, do not feel that you have to memorize all of the details. Simply remember where the information is located in the passage so that you can refer back to it in the future. A final type of passage will be a biographical account of some famous inventor or seminal figure in the field of plant operation. These passages are designed to be entertaining, and will likely include colorful descriptions and interesting anecdotes. When you are presented with a passage of this type, it is likely that you will be asked to describe the author's attitude towards his or her subject.

Now that we have covered the content areas from which the reading comprehension passages will be drawn, let us consider the types of questions that you will encounter. The first and most basic kind of reading comprehension question is the one that asks you to define the main idea of the passage. This question may arrive in any of a few different forms. The question may ask you for the "the best summary," the "general point," or the "overarching theme" of the passage. Do not be confused by the precise language: this is a main idea question. As you no doubt have learned by now, the main idea of a passage is most likely to appear in either the first or the last sentence. Therefore, as you are reading a passage for the first time, pay special attention to the beginning and end. Whether the main idea is offered first or last will depend on the type of passage: expository passages tend to give a main idea first and then spend the rest of the sentences defending it, while critical or argumentative essays will often begin with a set of loose facts and end with a summarizing conclusion. In any case, be prepared to refer back to the text in search of the main idea.

On occasion, the authors of the exam will try to fool you by asking you to provide the main idea of a specific *part* of the passage rather than of the passage as a whole. Similarly, they may try to confuse you with answer choices that are true without being the main idea of the passage. For this reason, it is imperative that you read the question carefully and do not just assume that the first or last sentence of the paragraph is the main idea. The main idea is not just any true statement contained within the passage: it is the idea that most effectively summarizes the entire passage.

It is certain that at least a couple of the reading comprehension questions will ask you to determine the main idea. In addition, it is quite likely that a few of the questions will ask you to recall specific details from the passage. This would appear to be the easiest kind of question to answer, but many students go astray by relying on memory instead of scrolling back up to find the pertinent details in the passage. Remember that you are free to refer to the text as much as you like. Also, remember that specific questions are likely to have specific answers, just as general questions are likely to have general answers. In other words, if the question asks you to name a concept, the answer probably will not be a piece of specific data.

A more subtle form of question is the one that requires you to diagnose the author's attitude. As with the main idea question, this kind of question can take a number of different forms. It may ask you to describe the "tone," "opinion," "feeling" or "mood" of the author or passage. All of these questions are essentially asking you to assess how the author feels about his or her topic. In order to answer such a question, you will have to pay attention to the specific language used by the author, and the point of view that the language conveys. For instance, if the author is describing a small person, he or she would create a sharply different tone by using the word *puny* than by using the word *petite*. *Puny* suggests a shriveled, scrawny individual, while *petite* conjures daintiness and delicacy. It may take a little bit of practice before you habitually notice these shades of meaning, but you should try to be conscious of the ways in which language can be used to subtly indicate attitude. For the most part, the test administrators avoid passages that are violently opinionated or controversial. Any answer choices that suggest the author holds an opinion which could be considered radical or offensive are most likely incorrect.

The final category of question which you may encounter on the exam is one that asks you to extend the author's reasoning. Put another way, these questions require you to consider the information provided in the passage and then use this information to consider a problem not mentioned in the passage. For example, a passage might describe the characteristics of a given community and the police activity that is recommended for that community. A question might then ask you to extend the reasoning of the author by describing the changes in police activity that could be made in response to a change in the community. The reasoning required to answer these kinds of questions will not be extremely complicated. The most common problem students have with questions asking them to extend the reasoning of the passage is that they attempt to find the answer explicitly in the passage. Remember that even though all of the information needed to answer every question can be found in the text, some questions will require you to do some independent thinking.

The best way to prepare for the reading comprehension section of the written examination is to practice reading a variety of different texts. By visiting the local library, you should be able to obtain journal articles, training manuals, written complaints, and persuasive essays on issues related to plant operation. As you read these texts, practice finding the main idea and identifying key details. You may want to practice scanning a short passage to determine the basic structure, before you go back and read in more detail. You will be allowed to make notes and underline on the written examination, so feel free to do this during your practice if it helps you to understand the text.

Mathematical Usage

Of all the tools a plant operator uses to perform his or her job effectively, perhaps the most important and the most forgotten is mathematics. In this era of calculators and computers, many people think that they will be able to attain professional success without achieving mathematical fluency. If one hopes to become a plant operator, however, there can be no substitute for a strong foundation of basic math skills. Plant operators have to make calculations, convert measurements, and organize numerical data on a daily basis. Many of the processes involved in the operation of a power plant are so subtle that they can only be measured quantitatively. For this reason, the POSS exam includes a mathematical usage section designed to assess your mastery of the fundamentals of arithmetic.

The mathematical usage section of the exam is short in comparison with other parts of the exam. It consists of 18 multiple-choice questions, which must be completed within seven minutes. These questions primarily pertain to arithmetic, though there may be some questions which require knowledge of basic algebra and geometry. The level of difficulty is approximately that of a sophomore- or junior-year math class in high school. So, with a little bit of a refresher, you should have no problem with this section of the exam.

The format of the mathematical usage questions should be familiar to you from other standardized tests. You will be asked to solve a problem, find the value of a variable, or provide some other piece of information. A great number of the questions will ask you to convert from one unit to another (for example, from inches to meters). Many of the mathematical usage questions will be word problems, in which you are asked to make a calculation based on the information given in a short passage. We will look at a couple of sample word problems a little later in this section.

Mathematical usage questions are in a multiple-choice format, with either four or five possible answers from which to choose. When these answer choices are real numbers without variables, they will usually be listed in order from least to greatest. One exception to this rule is when a question concerns the relative value of the answer choices. For instance, in a question asking you to select the greatest of a group of fractions, the answer choices will be listed in a random order.

Some of the mathematical usage questions will include graphs, charts, or geometric figures. Unless the exam specifies so, these drawings will not be perfectly accurate and to scale. You should never make any assumptions about a diagram on the exam; only consider information that is either explicitly given by the question or that can be calculated based on information explicitly given.

The most important thing to remember regarding mathematical usage questions is to read the question carefully and make sure you understand what it is asking. For instance, the exam is notorious for setting up an equation like $2x = 6$ and then asking you to solve for $x + 2$. Inevitably, many test takers will see the equation and simply solve for x; thus the exam punishes those who fail to read the question carefully. Therefore, before you even begin to solve the problem or examine the answer choices, make sure you know what the directions are asking you to do.

On many of the mathematical usage questions, the exam will not require the highest level of specificity. For instance, when the answer to a problem is a decimal with nine places, the answer choices will often round to the nearest hundredth or thousandth. Before you go to the trouble of working out the problem to the millionths place, take a look at the answer choices: you may be able to save yourself some labor.

Although calculators are not allowed on the exam, scratch paper and pencils will be made available. You should use this scratch paper as much as you can. Do not try to solve complicated problems in your head; put them down on paper so that you can get a visual sense and leave your mind free to work. The importance of scratch paper is true for the data sufficiency questions as well as the mathematical usage questions, but on the mathematical usage questions you should use the paper to solve each problem forwards and backwards. For instance, on a question that asks you to solve for a specific variable, you should solve for the variable, then plug that variable back into the original equation and make sure that it works. After you have reviewed basic arithmetic and algebra, you should have plenty of time to work out problems forwards and backwards on your scratch paper. By double checking your work in this way, you can prevent careless mistakes from lowering your score.

Let's consider an example of working backwards to solve a tricky mathematical usage question. Imagine that you are given the following scenario:

> *Brian takes an 81-inch piece of rope and cuts it three times. Each time he cuts the rope, he cuts off and discards the same fraction of the remaining length. When he is finished, the piece of rope is 3 inches long. Which fraction represents the amount of rope removed in each of the three cuts?*

This is a difficult question, and you may not know exactly how to approach it. This is when working backwards from the given answer choices can be an effective strategy. Let us imagine that the five answer choices for this problem are 1/8, 1/3, ½, 2/3, and ¾. When the answer choices are grouped in ascending order like this, it is a good idea to start with the middle value; if this answer is incorrect, you can often tell whether the right answer will be higher or lower.

So, returning to our example, let us begin with ½. If this is the correct answer, then the 3-inch rope left at the end of the problem would have been half the size of the rope remaining after two cuts. So, the amount of rope remaining after two cuts would be 6 inches. We can proceed on in this way: after one cut, the length of the rope would be 12 inches; before any cuts have been made, then, the length of the rope would be 24 inches. Obviously, since we know that the original length of the rope was 81 inches, ½ cannot be the correct answer. Furthermore, since plugging ½ into the problem yields an answer significantly smaller than we require, we can guess that the correct answer will be greater than ½.

Let us next consider 2/3, then. Remember that if 2/3 of the rope is cut off each time, the remaining amount will be 1/3 of the length before the cut. So, if the amount left after the third cut (3 inches) is 1/3 of the length of the rope before the third cut, the length of the rope before the third cut must be 9 inches (3 x 3 = 9). We can thus determine the preceding lengths of rope by multiplying by 3: before the second cut the length would have been 27 inches, and before the first cut, 81 inches. Aha! We can now be sure that 2/3 is the correct answer to the problem. Furthermore, we discovered this simply by working backwards from the answer choices given by the test.

There are some mathematical usage questions, however, for which it is not prudent to work both forwards and backwards. This is true of problems in which working backwards would require too much time and effort. On these problems, it may be more efficient to set up a basic algebraic equation to derive the information you need. For instance, consider the following problem:

> *Vincenzo's Gourmet Coffee sells medium roast beans for $7 a pound and dark roast beans for $6 a pound. If Denise orders a 12-pound mixture that costs $6.25 per pound, how many pounds of dark roast beans is she getting?*

The answer choices for this problem are 3, 6, 8, 9, and 10. Certainly, it would be possible to solve this problem by working backward. If you chose 8 as your starting point, you could multiply by 6 and add the product (48) to the product of the amount of medium roast beans and their cost per pound (4 x 7 = 28). You could then add these two products together and divide by 12 to determine the cost per pound of Denise's mixture: (48 + 28)/12 = $6.33. This is the wrong answer.

Obviously, you would have to go to a fair amount of trouble to calculate the answer this way. For this reason, it is better to set up an algebraic equation using the information given in the problem. The variable x will represent the number of dark roast beans in the mixture. The amount of medium roast beans can therefore be represented as $12 - x$. We know that the total cost of the dark roast beans in the mixture, $6x$, added to the total cost of the medium roast beans in the mixture, $7(12 - x)$, can be divided by the number of pounds of the mixture, 12, to yield the cost per pound, which we know to be $6.25. In other words, we can set up the following equation to find the number of pounds of dark roast beans in the mixture: $[6x + 7(12 - x)]/12 = 6.25$. Multiply both sides by 12, and then multiply the 7 across the parentheses, yielding: $6x + 84 - 7x = 75$. Simplify and subtract 84 from both sides to obtain: $-x = -9$. Make both sides of the equation positive to obtain: $x = 9$. Of course, developing and solving this equation has its perils, but it is far less time-consuming and less liable to careless error than working backward through a long series of calculations.

Finally, a few of the mathematical usage questions on your exam will include geometric figures. Some geometry-style problems will not be accompanied by a figure, and it will be in your best interest to draw one of your own on scratch paper. In either case, remember that you can only trust information about the figure that is explicitly given. The exam will usually try to draw figures to scale, but it does not always succeed, and therefore never make any assumptions about the relative sizes or angles of a figure. That being said, you can often derive some useful extra information from the values in the figure that are given. For instance, if you are given a square and told that one side is 6 inches long, you automatically know that all four sides are 6 inches long. Furthermore, you will know that every angle of the square is 90 degrees. This information may be required to find the answer to the problem.

The mathematical usage section of the exam is broken down into three main content areas: arithmetic, algebra, geometry. The vast majority of the mathematics questions will require you to perform basic calculations with whole numbers, fractions, and decimals. As mentioned earlier, the level of difficulty of this section of the exam should not exceed an eleventh-grade level. Following is an outline of all the specific topics included in the exam. (Note: Do not try to read this section at once! Either work through it paragraph by paragraph or use it as a reference for those topics that are unfamiliar or rusty. Space constraints prevent us from describing every topic exhaustively, so you may need to seek outside assistance on especially troublesome topics.)

Integers

Quite a few of the questions on the exam will require you to understand some of the basic properties of numbers, specifically integers. The set of numbers known as integers is composed of all the so-called counting numbers, both negative and positive, and including zero. So, expressed as a mathematical set, integers are {...-3, -2, -1, 0, 1, 2, 3...}. Fractions and decimals are not integers. Any integer that is a multiple of two is called an even integer; all other integers are considered to be odd. Zero is considered to be an even integer. Zero has some special properties: any number multiplied by zero will yield a product of zero, and it is not possible to divide a number by zero. Any groups of integers that are arranged in order from least to greatest, and without any gaps, are referred to as consecutive integers.

Place value

The value of an integer depends not only on the identity of the digits but on their placement. For instance, the numbers 0.61 and 0.061 are not the same. The position of a digit in a number is referred to as its place value. In order to answer some of the questions on the exam, you may need to be familiar with the more common place values. In a number that does not have a decimal point, the names of the place value increase by powers of ten as you move to the left. For instance, in the number 56,324, four is in the ones place, two is in the tens place, three is in the hundreds place, six is in the thousands place, and five is in the ten thousands place. It is easy to imagine how the progression of increasing places will continue: hundred thousands, millions, ten millions, etc. The place values on the right side of the decimal point also progress by powers of ten, beginning with tenths. As an example, in the number 0.5297, five is in the tenths place, two is in the hundredths place, nine is in the thousandths place, and seven is in the ten thousandths place. Again, it easy to imagine how these decreasing places will continue: hundred thousandths, millionths, ten millionths. Note that all of the place values to the right of the decimal point have a "th" at the end; make sure you don't confuse the thousands and the thousandths place on your exam.

Prime and composite numbers

Any number that can only be divided evenly by itself or one is a prime number. For example, three is a prime number because it can only be divided by three and one; four is not a prime number because it can be divided by two as well as by four and one. All numbers that are not prime numbers are referred to as composite numbers. Prime numbers are always positive, always whole numbers, and almost always odd (2 is the only even prime number).

Operations with integers

Arithmetic is basically just performing operations with integers. There are a few things to remember when working with negative integers. A good rule of thumb is to remember that two negatives equal a positive: subtracting a negative number is the same as adding it; multiplying or dividing two negative numbers yields a positive product or quotient. On the other hand, when only one of the terms in a multiplication or division product is negative, the resulting product or quotient will be negative as well. When one integer cannot be divided evenly into another, the number that is left over is called the remainder. For example, in the problem $5 \div 2$, two can go into five two times, with a remainder of one; this is expressed 2 r 1.

Factors and multiples

For any integer, the set of numbers which can be divided into that integer is known as its set of factors. Prime number will only have two factors: themselves and one. Composite number will have at least three factors: themselves, one, and some other number. The number 8, for example, has four factors: 8, 4, 2, and 1.

The multiples of an integer are all of the values produced when the integer is multiplied by another integer. The multiples of 3 are 3, 6, 9, 12, and so on. The multiples of 4 are 4, 8, 12, 16, 20, and so on.

Associative and distributive properties

There are a few basic arithmetic properties which, although they are unlikely to be specifically mentioned on the exam, may help you to figure out some other problems. The associative property of addition asserts that the order of the terms in an addition problem does not matter, and so the various terms can be grouped and organized in any way without affecting the total. As an example, (2 + 5) + 6 = 13; and 2 + (5 + 6) = 13. Also, for that matter, 2 + 6 + 5 = 13, and 5 + 6 + 2 = 13. As long as the terms in an addition problem do not change, the sum will not change either.

In a similar vein, the associative property of multiplication asserts that the grouping of the terms in a multiplication problem will not affect the product. So, for example, 5 (2 x 3) = 30, 3 (2 x 5) = 30, 3 x 2 x 5 = 30, 5 x 2 x 3 = 30, and so on.

The distributive law is only slightly more complicated. It states that any number multiplied by a set of values within parentheses is multiplied by every value within the parentheses. To illustrate, 3 (5 + 4) = 3(5) + 3(4). Occasionally, the exam will ask you to transform a problem in the opposite way, as follows: 3(17) + 3 (14) = 3 (17 + 14). The problem may even be written in a slightly more confusing manner, such as: 5(12) – 83(5) = 5 (12 – 83).

Absolute value

The absolute value of a number is its distance from zero. Absolute value is denoted by two vertical lines. Since absolute value is the measure of distance, it cannot be negative. So, the absolute value of 6, written |6|, is 6, and the absolute value of -6 is 6 as well.

Fractions

A fraction, for instance ½, consists of a numerator on top and a denominator on the bottom. Fractions are said to be equivalent when they can be reduced to be the same thing; for example, 5/10 is equivalent to ½, because it can be reduced to ½ by dividing both numerator and denominator by 5. Remember that when reducing a fraction you must divide numerator and denominator by the same number. In order to perform addition or subtraction operations with fractions, you must have a common denominator. Once you have a common denominator, you simply perform the operation with the numerators, leaving the denominators alone. To multiply two fractions, multiply the numerators together and then multiply the denominators together. To divide one fraction by another, invert the second fraction and then multiply first numerators and then denominators. A fraction in which the numerator is greater than the denominator is called an improper fraction. An expression consisting of a whole number and a fraction—for instance 5 ½—is called a mixed number.

Decimals

Decimals, like fractions, are a way of expressing values other than integers. Indeed, every fraction has an equivalent decimal: for instance, the fraction ¼ is equivalent to the decimal 0.25. When working with decimals, it is very important to understand how different operations affect the number of places to the right of the decimal point. When adding or subtracting decimals, the resulting sum or difference should have as many decimal places as the term in the operation with the most decimal places. In the problem 1.5 + 1.05, for example, the answer must have two numbers to the right of the decimal point. One way to simplify such problems is to add zeroes to the ends of those numbers with fewer decimal places; for instance, making our example 1.50 + 1.05. When two decimals are multiplied together, the resulting product will have the sum of the decimal places in the two terms. In other words, the product of 3.55 x 4.785 will have five places to the right of the decimal point, because the first term has two and the second term has three. In order to divide decimals, the divisor must be converted into an integer by moving the decimal point to the right. So, in order to complete the problem 5.55 ÷ 2.8, we would need to shift the decimal point in both terms one place to the right, resulting in the problem 55.5 ÷ 28. The resulting quotient will have one place to the right of the decimal point.

> **Review Video: Integers, Decimals, and Fractions**
> *Visit **mometrix.com/academy** and enter **Code: 688110***

Exponents

When the number is multiplied by itself several times, we use a form of notation called an exponent. For instance, the number 2^5 is expressed verbally as "two to the fifth power," and is equivalent to 2 x 2 x 2 x 2 x 2. When a number is raised to the second power (that is, when its exponent is 2), we say that the number is being "squared." When a number is raised to the third power (exponent is 3), we say that the number is being "cubed." For any number, an exponent of zero makes the number equal to 1. When the number has a negative exponent, is equal to one over the number raised to the absolute value of the exponent; in other words, $x^{-1} = 1/x$; $x^{-2} = 1/x^2$; $x^{-3} = 1/x^3$ ...

Operations with exponents

There are specific rules for multiplying and dividing numbers with exponents. When two terms with the same base are multiplied together, as for example 2^3 x 2^4, the exponents are added together: 2^3 x 2^4 = 2^7. When two terms with different bases but the same exponent are multiplied together, as in 2^3 x 3^3, only the two bases are multiplied: 2^3 x 3^3 = 6^3. When the same base is given two exponents, as in $(3^2)^3$, the exponents are multiplied together: $(3^2)^3$ = 3^6. When two terms with the same base but different exponents are involved in a division problem, as in $3^4/3^2$, the exponent in the denominator is subtracted from the exponent in the numerator: $3^4/3^2$ = 3^2. Finally, when a fraction is given an exponent, as in $(3/4)^2$, the exponent applies to both the numerator and the denominator: $(3/4)^2$ = $3^2/4^2$.

> ➤ **Review Video: Exponents**
> *Visit **mometrix.com/academy** and enter **Code: 629918***

Square roots

The number that when multiplied by itself would produce a given number is called the "square root" of that given number; for instance, 2 is the square root of 4, since 2 x 2 = 4. Note that -2 could also be considered a square root of 4, since -2 x -2 = 4. Every positive number will have two square roots, one of which will be negative. Also, because any positive or negative number multiplied by itself has a positive product, negative numbers do not have square roots. (This will probably not come up on the exam, but the square root of 0 is 0, because 0^2 = 0). The standard notation for, say, the square root of two is $\sqrt{2}$. If a question is specifically asking for the negative square root of 2, this is expressed $-\sqrt{2}$. When two square roots are multiplied together, the numbers are simply multiplied and the resulting product remains as a square root: $\sqrt{2}$ x $\sqrt{3}$ = $\sqrt{6}$. In like fashion, when one square root is divided by another, the terms inside the root symbol are divided and the square root sign is left intact: $\sqrt{8}/\sqrt{4}$ = $\sqrt{2}$.

> ➤ **Review Video: Square Roots**
> *Visit **mometrix.com/academy** and enter **Code: 648063***

Order of operations

There is a specific order in which the various components of an arithmetic problem must be performed. This system is known as the order of operations, and is as follows: parentheses, exponents, multiplication, division, addition, and subtraction. The order of operations is easy to follow if you just remember the mnemonic phrase "Please excuse my dear Aunt Sally." The first letters of the words in this sentence (Please Excuse My Dear Aunt Sally) mirror those of the order of operations: Parentheses, Exponents, Multiplication, Division, Addition, and Subtraction. So, as an example, take a look at the following arithmetic expression: $3(4 + 3^2)$ – 2. In order to derive the correct answer, you would need to begin by determining the value of the parentheses, first by calculating the exponent 3^2, and then by adding 4. Next, you would multiply by 3 (because multiplication preceded subtraction in the order of operations), and finally you would subtract 2. The correct value of this expression is 37. Note that if you tried to calculate the value of this expression without observing the proper order of operations (say, by subtracting 2 from the parentheses before multiplying by 3) you would not find the same answer.

> ➢ **Review Video:** Order of Operations
> *Visit **mometrix.com/academy** and enter **Code: 275605***

Percents

When a number is expressed as a percentage, this means that it is being expressed as a portion of 100. So, 25% is equivalent to 25 hundredths, or 0.25. Another way to express this is as a fraction: 25/100. If you prefer, you can always convert the percentages on the exam into decimals or fractions. The most common kind of percentage problem you will see on the exam is one that asks you to find a certain percentage of the given number. These problems are easily solved by multiplying the decimal equivalent of the percentage by the given number. As an example, imagine you are asked to calculate 25% of 40; you would simply multiply 0.25 by 40, resulting in an answer of 10 (remember the rules for multiplying decimals!). A similar kind of question will ask you to determine what percentage of a given number another number is. For instance, a question might ask what percentage of 40 the number 8 is. The way to solve this kind of problem is to set up a proportional equation as follows: $8/40 = x/100$. This equation can be expressed as "8 is to 40 as x is to 100." Such an equation can then be solved by cross multiplying and solving for x, yielding an answer of 20%.

Ratios

Another name for the proportion on either side of the last percentage equation is ratio. A ratio is simply a comparison between numbers. Indeed, ratios are noted in the same way as verbal analogies, as both involve a consideration of the relationship between two things. The ratio 4 to 5, then, would be expressed 4:5. Ratios can also be expressed as fractions: for example, 4/5. Some ratios can be simplified. For instance, in the ratio 8:12, both terms are divisible by 4, so we can simplify the ratio to 2:3.

> ➢ **Review Video:** Ratios and Percentages
> *Visit **mometrix.com/academy** and enter **Code: 904334***

Lines and angles

The basic unit of geometry is the line. Unless it is specified otherwise, lines are assumed to travel in opposite directions infinitely. Lines that are finite are called line segments. Where two lines intersect, angles are formed. The exam will require you to know a few of the basic types of angles. A right angle is one in which the two sides of the angle are perpendicular to one another; a right angle measures 90°. An acute angle has a measure between 0° and 90°. An obtuse angle has a measure between 90° and 180°. An angle with a measure of 180° is called a straight angle, although for all intents and purposes this is just a straight line. Two or more angles that add up to 90° are referred to as complementary angles. Two or more angles that add up to 180° are referred to as supplementary angles. There is no such thing as a negative angle, or an angle measuring 0°. When two lines intersect and form 4 angles, the angles opposite one another are referred to as vertical angles; vertical angles are always equal. When two parallel lines (i.e., lines extending infinitely in either direction but never touching) are intersected by a third line, known as a transversal, the corresponding angles formed are called transverse angles.

> ➢ **Review Video:** <u>Angles</u>
> *Visit* ***mometrix.com/academy*** *and enter* ***Code:* 831357**

Triangles

There are a few properties and varieties of triangles that you will need to know for the exam. In every triangle, the largest angle is opposite the longest side. The sum of the lengths of the two smallest sides of a triangle will be greater than the length of the longest side. When the measures of the angles inside a triangle are added up, the sum is always 180°. A triangle with three equal sides into three equal angles is known as an equilateral triangle. A triangle with two equal angles and two equal sides is referred to as an isosceles triangle. A triangle that has no equal sides and no equal angles is referred to as a scalene triangle. Any triangle in which one angle is equal to 90° is called a right triangle. In such a triangle, the two sides that form the right angle are called the legs, and the other side is called the hypotenuse. The Pythagorean theorem describes one unique property of right triangles: the sum of the squares of the lengths of the two legs is equal to the length of the hypotenuse squared. This is usually written as follows: $a^2 + b^2 = c^2$. Remember that the Pythagorean theorem only works for right triangles.

Quadrilaterals and other polygons

A quadrilateral is any figure with four sides, in which the four interior angles add up to 360°. There are a few special quadrilaterals. A quadrilateral with four equal sides and four right angles is called a square. A quadrilateral with four equal sides and four interior angles that are not equal is called a rhombus. A quadrilateral with four equal angles and two opposite and equal pairs of sides is called a rectangle. All the angles in a rectangle are right angles. A quadrilateral with two opposite and equal pairs of sides and two opposite and equal pairs of non-right angles is called a parallelogram. A quadrilateral with four unequal angles and one pair of parallel sides is called a trapezoid.

Triangles and quadrilaterals are the types of polygons (closed figures) you are most likely to encounter on the exam. You should know the names of some other regular polygons, however. A regular polygon is one in which all the sides and all the angles are equal. A regular polygon with five sides is called a pentagon, one with six sides is called a hexagon, one with seven sides is called a heptagon, one with eight sides is called an octagon, one with nine sides is called a nonagon and one with ten sides is called a decagon. There is a simple formula for determining the sum of the interior angles in a regular polygon: simply subtract two from the number of sides and multiply by 180°; this is most often written as: *(n-2)180°* . The sum of the interior angles of a pentagon, for instance, would be (5 – 2) 180° = 540°. You can find the measure of each interior angle by dividing the sum of the interior angles by the number of sides in the figure: 540°/5 = 108°.

Circles

In geometry, a circle is defined as all of the points in a plane that are the same distance from a given point (the center of the circle). The distance from the center of a circle to any point on its border is known as the radius. Any line that passes from one edge of the circle to another is called a chord. The length of a line extending from one edge of the circle to another and passing through the center is known as the diameter. The diameter is the longest chord in any given circle. The diameter of a circle is twice the radius. The distance around the edge of the circle is known as the circumference of the circle. The circumference of a circle can be determined with the following equation: $c = 2\pi r$, in which r is the radius of the circle. The set of points including and connecting any two points on the edge of the circle is called an arc of the circle. Like angles, arcs are measured in degrees; the largest possible arc is 360°. Any line that intersects with a circle in exactly one point is called a tangent of that circle. The radius running from the center of the circle to the point at which a tangent intersects the edge of the circle will be perpendicular to the tangent. Two or more circles that share a center but have different diameters are referred to as concentric circles.

Area and perimeter

You will need to know a few basic formulae for calculating the area of various figures. The area of the triangle is calculated: *a = ½(base x height),* where the base is one side of the triangle and the height runs perpendicular to the base. The perimeter of the triangle, and indeed the perimeter of any polygon, is the sum of the lengths of the sides. The area of a square, rectangle, or parallelogram can be calculated by multiplying the length by the width. The area of a rhombus can be calculated by multiplying one half by the product of the two diagonals (lines drawn between the vertices of opposing angles). The area of a circle is found: $a = \pi r^2$, in which r is the radius of the circle.

> ➤ **Review Videos: <u>Areas in Geometry</u>**
> *Visit **mometrix.com/academy** and enter **Code: 663492***

Cylinders, rectangular solids, and cubes

Occasionally, the exam will require you to work with basic three-dimensional figures like cubes, cylinders, and rectangular solids. A cylinder (shaped like a can) has two parallel circular bases of equal diameter. The height of a cylinder is measured perpendicular to the bases. The surface area of a cylinder is measured with the equation $A = 2(\pi r^2) + 2\pi rh$, in which r is the radius of the bases and h is the height. The volume of a cylinder can be calculated with the equation $V = \pi r^2 h$. A rectangular solid (shaped like a box) has six faces and twelve edges, connected at eight vertices. The volume of a rectangular solid is calculated with the equation $V = lwh$, in which l is length, w is width, and h is height. If these three measures are equal, the rectangular sold is called a cube. The surface area of a rectangular solid is calculated with the equation $A = 2(wl + lh + wh)$; in other words, surface area is the sum of the areas of the six faces of the rectangular solid.

> ➤ **Review Video: <u>Cube</u>**
> *Visit **mometrix.com/academy** and enter **Code: 664455***

> ➤ **Review Video: <u>Cylinder</u>**
> *Visit **mometrix.com/academy** and enter **Code: 226463***

Mean, median, mode

Some questions on the exam may present you with a set of data and ask you to name the mean, median, or mode of the set. The mean of a set is the same thing as the average, and is calculated in the same way, namely by adding together all the values in the set and dividing by the number of values in the set. For instance, then, in the set of data {5, 6, 4, 9}, the mean would be calculated as follows: $(5 + 6 + 4 + 9)/4 = 6$. The median of a set is the middle value when the set is arranged from least to greatest. Therefore, in the set {1, 3, 5}, the median is 3. If the set contains an even number of values, the median is calculated by adding together the 2 middle values and dividing by 2. So, for the set {2, 4, 6, 8}, the median would be calculated: (4 + 6)/2 = 5. Finally, the mode of a set of data is the value within the set that occurs most frequently. Sometimes, a set will have more than one mode, or, if every value within the set appears only once, it will not really have a mode at all.

> ➢ **Review Video:** <u>Mean, Median, and Mode</u>
> *Visit **mometrix.com/academy** and enter **Code: 286207***

Range and standard deviation

For any given set of values, the range is the distance from the greatest value to the least. This can be calculated by subtracting the least value from the greatest. So, for the set {2, 5, 7, 8, 12), the range would be calculated 12 – 2 = 10. The method of calculating range is not affected by the number of values in the set, or by the number of values that share the least or greatest measure.

Calculating the range is a rather crude way of judging the dispersion of values in a set of data. A more sophisticated measure is standard deviation. The process of determining standard deviation has several steps. First, the arithmetic mean of the set must be calculated. Next, the difference between each member of the set and the arithmetic mean must be found, and these differences must be squared and added together. This sum is then divided by the number of values in the set, and the square root of the quotient is found. This is defined by the formula:

$$\sigma = \sqrt{\frac{\left[\sum_{i=1}^{N}(x_i - \mu)^2\right]}{N}}$$

where σ (sigma) is the standard deviation, x_i is the particular value in question, μ (mu) is the average of the set of values and N is the total number of values in the set. One thus sees that the standard deviation is the absolute value of this square root (because standard deviation cannot be negative). Although it is unlikely that you will be required to calculate the standard deviation for a set of data, you should still have a working knowledge of the method for calculating standard deviation. It is more typical for a question to give you the mean and the standard deviation of a set, and then to ask you to determine the range of a certain number of standard deviations from the mean.

For example, say a set of data has a mean of 6 and a standard deviation of 2. If you are asked to calculate the range of values within 2 standard deviations of the mean, you can do so by first multiplying the standard deviation by 2. Standard deviation extends to either side of the arithmetic mean, so the range will be all the values within 4 on either side of the mean. In other words, the range of values within 2 standard deviations of 6 will be 2 through 10.

➢ **Review Video: Range**
Visit ***mometrix.com/academy*** *and enter* ***Code: 778133***

Average

The word *average* is synonymous with the word *median*. The basic rule for finding the average of a set of data is to add up all the members of the set and then divide by the number of members. The average of a set containing 1, 3, 6, and 6 would be calculated: (1 + 3 + 6 + 6)/4 = 4.

Some problems will give you the average of an incomplete set of data and ask you to identify the missing term. You can solve this kind of problem by rearranging the equation for finding an average. Instead of average = sum/# of members, use sum = average x # of members. So for instance, if you are told that the average of a set containing 7, 5, x, and 20 is 10, you can determine that the sum of the members of the set must be 10 x 4 = 40. Since the known members of the set add up to 32, the missing member of the set must be 8.

On rare occasions, you may have to deal with weighted averages, in which some of the values in the set are given more importance than others. For example, imagine that during the last ten games a certain baseball team scored 8 runs one time, 4 runs three times, 2 runs five times, and 0 runs one time. You could not simply add up 8, 4, 2, and 0 and divide by 4 to find the average number of runs scored over the last ten games. Instead, you need to set the number of members of the set as ten, and then multiply each value by its number of occurrences before adding. Therefore, the average would be calculated as follows: [1(8) + 3(4) + 5(2) + 1(0)]/10 = 3.

➢ **Review Video: Average**
Visit ***mometrix.com/academy*** *and enter* ***Code: 176521***

Distance, rate, and time

Probably the most common type of word problem on the exam is the one that asks you to consider distance, rate, and time. You will recognize these problems; they begin with something like, "John drives 3 hours at 50 miles per hour. How many miles does John drive?" In other words, two values are given and you are asked to find the third. This is easy enough when you remember the simple equation *distance = rate* x *time*. In the example problem, the rate is 50 mph and the time is 3 hours, ergo the distance is 150 miles. Always make sure that the units in the problem are consistent, as you will not get very far trying to convert kilometers per hour into miles. Also, be aware that the unknown variable will not always be distance, in which case you will need to rearrange the equation to solve for rate or time. For instance, if the problem states that "Dale drives 75 miles at 25 miles per hour," and asks you to determine how many hours Dale has been driving, you will need to solve for t, and thus your equation will be $t = d/r$. If the problem asks you to solve for rate, the equation will need to be rearranged to $r = d/t$.

> ➤ **Review Video: Distance**
> Visit *mometrix.com/academy* and enter *Code:* **186126**

Interest problems

Some word problems will require you to calculate the amount of interest that accrues on a given amount of money over a certain amount of time. In order to solve these problems, you will need to know the equation $I = prt$, in which I is interest, p is principle, r is rate of interest and t is time. Imagine the following scenario: $20 is placed into an account with an annual interest rate of 5%. How much interest will the money have accrued over 5 years? The principal is $20, the interest rate is 5% (for the purposes of calculation you will want to convert the percentage into a decimal, so 5% becomes 0.05), and the time is 5, so the equation can be set up: $I = 20$ x 0.05 x 5, yielding an answer of $5. Remember to make sure that if the interest rate is annual, the time needs to be in units of years as well (for instance, six months would become 0.5). Do not worry about compound interest or variable rates; the interest-related questions on the exam do not get so complex.

> ➤ **Review Video: Interest**
> Visit *mometrix.com/academy* and enter *Code:* **559176**

Graphs

The graphs used on the exam will be of the kinds most familiar to students: circle/pie graph, double axis line graph, triple axis line graph, and bar graph. Remember that on a circle or pie graph, the circle itself represents 1, or 100%. A double axis graph, otherwise known as a line graph, has a horizontal and a vertical axis, each of which represent an individual variable. A triple axis graph has an additional vertical axis on the right side, which is used to mark a third variable. A bar graph is composed of vertical or horizontal bars representing certain values. In rare cases, a question may include two kinds of graphs. When confronting this sort of problem, be sure that the units and scale used by the two graphs are consistent. If they are not, you will need to make adjustments in order to make accurate comparisons of data from each of the graphs.

> ➤ **Review Video:** <u>Graphs</u>
> *Visit **mometrix.com/academy** and enter **Code: 355505***

Measurement conversions

It is very likely that you will confront a few questions asking you to convert one kind of unit(s) into another. At the beginning of the exam, you will be given a list of several equivalencies: 12 inches = 1 foot, 3 feet = 1 yard, 1 centimeter = 0.394 inches, etc. You may then be asked to convert a given amount in one unit to the same amount in another unit. Some of these will be very easy, as for instance: *Convert 3 feet into inches.* To solve this and other problems of this type, simply set up a ratio equation: 1 foot/12 inches = 3 feet/x inches. This equation says, 1 foot is to twelve inches as 3 feet is to x number of inches. To solve, simply cross multiply to derive: x = 36. In other words, 3 feet is equal to 36 inches.

On occasion, you will be given a problem that requires you to make more than one step. For instance, using the equivalencies listed above, consider the following question: how many centimeters are in two feet? We do not have a direct equivalency between feet and centimeters, so we will have to make two steps: convert feet into inches and inches into centimeters. The first equation is easy: 1 foot/12 inches = 2 feet/ x inches. Cross-multiplying, we end up with 2 feet = 24 inches. Now, we can set up a similar equation to convert inches into centimeters: 0.394 inches/1 centimeter = 24 inches/x centimeters. Because of the decimal, this calculation will be a bit messier, but cross-multiplying should yield: $0.394x = 24$. Now, both sides of the equation must be divided by 0.394, yielding roughly 61. In other words, 2 feet = 24 inches = 61 centimeters. When confronted with a problem like this that requires you to take more than one step, remember to go slow and break the problem down into its component parts.

Practice Test

Mathematical Usage

Use the following information to answer questions 1-18:

1 acre = 43,560 square feet
1 barrel = 42 gallons
1 fathom = 6 feet
1 foot = 12 inches
1 furlong = 40 rods
1 gallon = 3.785 liters
1 gallon = 4 quarts
1 hand = 10 centimeters
1 inch = 2.54 centimeters
1 kilogram = 1,000 grams
1 kilogram = 2.2 pounds
1 kilometer = 1,000 meters
1 mile = 1.609 kilometers
1 mile = 5,280 feet
3 mile/hour = 4.4 feet/second
1 pint = 4 gills
1 pound = 16 ounces
1 quart = 2 pints
1 slug = 14.59 kilograms
1 square mile = 640 acres

If none of the answers listed are correct, select answer e, N for none of the above.

1. 6 kilograms = ? pounds
    a. 2.2
    b. 6,000
    c. 15.2
    d. 13.2
    e. N

2. 4 furlongs = ? rods
    a. 160
    b. 10
    c. 40
    d. 0.1
    e. N

3. 80 ounces = ? pounds
   a. 5
   b. 16
   c. 8
   d. 10
   e. N

4. 3 acres = ? square feet
   a. 43,560
   b. 1,920
   c. 130,680
   d. 640
   e. N

5. 2 miles = ? kilometers
   a. 1.609
   b. 3.218
   c. 1.243
   d. 2.486
   e. N

6. 3 quart = ? gallons
   a. 0.33
   b. 4
   c. 1.33
   d. 0.75
   e. N

7. 12 fathoms = ? feet
   a. 2
   b. 12
   c. 72
   d. 6
   e. N

8. 126 gallons = ? barrels
   a. 3
   b. 4
   c. 42
   d. 5292
   e. N

9. 60 miles/hour = ? feet/second
    a. 5
    b. 100
    c. 41
    d. 88
    e. N

10. 500 grams = ? kilograms
    a. 500,000
    b. 0.5
    c. 50
    d. 0.05
    e. N

11. 15 hands = ? centimeters
    a. 38
    b. 1.5
    c. 60
    d. 150
    e. N

12. 15.14 liters = ? gallons
    a. 2
    b. 3
    c. 4
    d. 5
    e. N

13. 2 barrels = ? quarts
    a. 336
    b. 21
    c. 168
    d. 672
    e. N

14. 1 mile = ? centimeters
    a. 849,733,632
    b. 160,934
    c. 13,411
    d. 30.5
    e. N

15. 13.2 pounds = ? grams
    a. 6
    b. 60
    c. 600
    d. 6,000
    e. N

16. 8 fathoms = ? inches
    a. 96
    b. 48
    c. 576
    d. 4,608
    e. N

17. 8 quarts = ? liters
    a. 7.57
    b. 121.12
    c. 15.14
    d. 0.53
    e. N

18. 5 feet = ? centimeters
    a. 12.7
    b. 23.6
    c. 152.4
    d. 60
    e. N

In problems 19-32, solve for X in the equation given.

19. $8X + 5 = 61$ $X = ?$
    a. 4
    b. 6
    c. 7
    d. 8
    e. N

20. $\frac{X}{3} = \frac{X}{6} + 4$ $X = ?$
    a. 9
    b. 12
    c. 18
    d. 24
    e. N

21. $3X - 15 = -2X$ $X = ?$
   a. 2
   b. 3
   c. 5
   d. 6
   e. N

22. $\frac{0.5}{X} - 0.8 = \frac{0.7}{X}$ $X = ?$
   a. -1
   b. -0.5
   c. -0.25
   d. 1
   e. N

23. $0.4X + 1.6 = 1$ $X = ?$
   a. -4
   b. -2.5
   c. -2
   d. -1.5
   e. N

24. $\frac{X}{0.4} + 0.5 = 2.5$ $X = ?$
   a. 0.8
   b. 1
   c. 2
   d. 4
   e. N

25. $5X - 0.9 - .5X$ $X - ?$
   a. 0.1
   b. 0.2
   c. 0.5
   d. 2
   e. N

26. $\frac{1}{X} - 0.2 = 0.3$ $X = ?$
   a. 0.2
   b. 0.5
   c. 2
   d. 5
   e. N

27. $0.8X = 6 + 0.4X$ $X = ?$
   a. 1.5
   b. 2.5
   c. 12
   d. 15
   e. N

28. $\frac{2}{X} = \frac{1}{X} + 2$ $X = ?$
   a. 0.3
   b. 0.5
   c. 0.6
   d. 1
   e. N

29. $X - 42 = -6X$ $X = ?$
   a. 7
   b. 8
   c. 12
   d. 21
   e. N

30. $\frac{4}{X} - 6 = -\frac{0.2}{X}$ $X = ?$
   a. 0.3
   b. 0.4
   c. 0.6
   d. 0.7
   e. N

31. $2X + 5 = 11$ $X = ?$
   a. 3
   b. 5
   c. 6
   d. 8
   e. N

32. $\frac{X}{0.2} - 4 = 16$ $X = ?$
   a. 2
   b. 4
   c. 6
   d. 8
   e. N

Use the following information to answer questions 33-46:

Perimeter of a square = 4 × side length
Perimeter of a rectangle = 2 × length + 2 × width
Circumference of a circle = 2 × π × radius
(π ≈ 3.14)

Area of a square = (side length)^2
Area of a rectangle = length × width
Area of a parallelogram = base × height
Area of a triangle = base × height/2
Area of a circle = π × (radius)^2

Volume of a prism or cylinder = (area of base) × height
Volume of a pyramid or cone = [(area of base) × height]/3
Volume of a sphere = 4/3 × π × (radius)^3

Density of an object = mass/volume

Degrees Fahrenheit (°F) = °C × 1.8 + 32
Degrees Celsius (°C) = (°F – 32)/1.8
Degrees Rankine (°R) = °F + 459.67
Kelvin (K) = °C + 273.15

33. A merry-go-round has a circular fence around it to keep people at a safe distance. The radius of the circular fence is 10 meters. How many meters long is the fence?
   a. 31.4
   b. 62.8
   c. 78.5
   d. 314
   e. N

34. A temperature gauge on the side of a process pipe reads 45 °C. What is the temperature in degrees Fahrenheit?
   a. 7.22
   b. 49
   c. 113
   d. 318.15
   e. N

35. What would be the volume of a cylindrical tank with a height of 150 feet and a radius of 30 feet?

    a. 28,274

    b. 106,029

    c. 424,115

    d. 563,231

    e. N

36. Jim is trying to decide how much paint he needs to paint his garage. Each of the four walls he wants to paint is 20 feet long and 9 feet high. If each can of paint covers 120 square feet of wall, how many cans of paint will he need to paint his garage?

    a. 1

    b. 3

    c. 5

    d. 6

    e. N

37. A rectangular plot of land has an area of 250,000 square feet. If one side of the plot is 400 feet long, how long is the adjacent side?

    a. 250

    b. 350

    c. 500

    d. 625

    e. N

38. The freezing point of a particular chemical is listed as -80 °C. What is the freezing point in Kelvin?

    a. 193.15

    b. 379.67

    c. -112

    d. 353.15

    e. N

39. A rectangular cereal box is being redesigned to improve its shelf profile, while keeping the same volume as before. Its depth is increasing from 2 inches to 2.5 inches, and its width is increasing from 10 inches to 12 inches. If its current height is 18 inches, what will the new height be?

    a. 10

    b. 12

    c. 15

    d. 18

    e. N

40. A pyramid with a square base has a volume of 4,800,000 cubic feet. If its height is 160 feet, how long is each side of the base?
    a. 100
    b. 120
    c. 150
    d. 160
    e. N

41. The boiling point of a certain chemical is found to be 250 °F. What would this boiling point be in Kelvin?
    a. 121.11
    b. 394.26
    c. 523.15
    d. 580.78
    e. N

42. A farmer has a rectangular field, 10,000 feet by 2500 feet, where he grows corn. He can grow the same amount of corn in a nearby square field, but he needs to put a fence around the corn in this field to keep his animals out. How long of a fence will the farmer need?
    a. 20,000
    b. 25,000
    c. 50,000
    d. 100,000
    e. N

43. A round marble has a mass of 50 grams and a radius of 1 centimeter. What is the density of the marble in grams per cubic centimeter?
    a. 11.94
    b. 15.92
    c. 50
    d. 157.08
    e. N

44. The autoignition temperature of a particular fuel source is 685 °F. What is the equivalent temperature in degrees Rankine?
    a. 225.33
    b. 362.78
    c. 958.15
    d. 1144.67
    e. N

45. A large funnel (inverted cone) can hold up to 90,000 cubic centimeters of liquid at a time. If the funnel has a height of 60 centimeters, how wide is the base (diameter)?

    a. 37.9
    b. 44.7
    c. 50.5
    d. 75.7
    e. N

46. A liquid chemical with constant density is stored in two spherical tanks. One tank has a radius of 5 feet, while the other has a radius of 10 feet. Both tanks are completely filled with the liquid. If the smaller tank can hold 10,000 kg of the chemical, how many kg can the larger tank hold?

    a. 20,000
    b. 40,000
    c. 80,000
    d. 120,000
    e. N

Reading for Comprehension

Passage #1

A hydroelectric power plant uses the potential energy of water to generate electricity. These facilities must be located next to a large body of water, whether natural or man-made. The amount of energy that can be developed by the plant is directly proportional to the volume of water at the site, as well as the rate at which the water is allowed to flow through the plant. In a typical arrangement, the power plant is built atop or alongside a dam, through which water is permitted to flow at a controlled pace. This water flow spins turbines that are attached to alternators, which generate the electrical power.

Hydroelectric power plants have many wonderful qualities relative to other plants. They are very clean and are inexpensive to operate and maintain. Hydroelectric plants are also very reliable and can move from inaction to operation at full capacity in a matter of minutes. These plants can be operated with a great deal of precision, which promotes efficiency. Finally, hydroelectric plants are considered to be one of the most durable systems, which means that they maintain their efficiency throughout their lives.

Unfortunately, hydroelectric power plants have specific demands that can be difficult to meet. They require a long area, and they cost a great deal of money to construct. They also tend to have long transmission lines, so they are subject to a number of inefficiencies. Perhaps the most negative aspect of a hydroelectric power plant is not associated with the plant itself, but with the large reservoir of water that must be alongside the plant. These reservoirs submerge huge amounts of land and can have devastating effects on wildlife and human settlements alike. Moreover, hydroelectric power plants are dependent on the water supply, so prolonged droughts can make it impossible for these facilities to operate.

Clearly, hydroelectric power plants cannot be built just anywhere. The best sites for these plants are large lakes at high altitude, especially in areas that receive a great deal of rainfall. It is good for the land to be rocky, because this will make it better able to support the heavy equipment that must be used in construction and operation. Also, it is important for there to be adequate roads or rails to move all of this equipment. All of these requirements mean that only a few sites will be truly appropriate for a hydroelectric power plant.

1. Which phrase from the passage best illustrates that a hydroelectric plant should be placed next to a large body of water?
    a. "The amount of energy that can be developed by the plant is directly proportional to the volume of water at the site."
    b. "These reservoirs submerge huge amounts of land and can have devastating effects on wildlife and human settlements alike."
    c. "In a typical arrangement, the power plant is built atop or alongside a dam, through which water is permitted to flow at a controlled pace."
    d. "Hydroelectric power plants are dependent on the water supply."

2. In a hydroelectric power plant, what do the alternators do?
    a. cool the water
    b. generate the electrical power
    c. maintain efficiency
    d. spin the turbines

3. Which of the following is NOT an advantage of hydroelectric power plants?
    a. They are clean
    b. They are inexpensive to operate
    c. They are durable
    d. They are inexpensive to construct

4. What does it mean in the second paragraph when it says that "Hydroelectric power plants have many wonderful qualities relative to other plants"?
    a. Hydroelectric power plants have many similarities with other plants.
    b. Hydroelectric power plants have many advantages over other plants.
    c. Hydroelectric power plants have many disadvantages compared to other plants.
    d. Hydroelectric power plants have many differences from other plants.

5. Based on the information in the passage, which of the following is probably true?
    a. Most hydroelectric power plants are built on sandy soil.
    b. Hydroelectric power plants must be built next to natural bodies of water.
    c. Hydroelectric plants are more expensive to operate than nuclear plants.
    d. An old hydroelectric power plant is approximately as efficient as a new one.

6. Why is rocky soil better for a hydroelectric power plant?
    a. The rocks can be used to build the plant.
    b. It is better at supporting heavy equipment.
    c. Rocky soil tends to contain less vegetation.
    d. Bodies of water are usually surrounded by rocky soil.

7. The last paragraph of the passage deals primarily with
   a. the selection of a site for a hydroelectric power plant.
   b. the need for rocky soil under a hydroelectric power plant
   c. the advantages of hydroelectric power plants
   d. the disadvantages of hydroelectric power plants

Passage #2

Nuclear power is produced in reactors. The chain reaction created inside a reactor is an example of controlled fission, because the intensity of the reaction and the amount of energy produced are carefully modulated. The fission in a nuclear reactor is also continuous, which means that there is an ever-present risk of accident. In order for nuclear power plants to function safely, the reactor core must be cooled constantly.

The production of electricity in a nuclear power plant requires sufficient raw material. In most cases, the fuel is a naturally occurring isotope of uranium, U-235. This isotope is fairly common, but for the purpose of nuclear power production it must be present in very large amounts, which requires purification and concentration until at least 3% of the material is U-235. Once enough of this material has been created, the uranium is molded into standardized, consistent units. These are typically cylindrical pellets with a thickness of about a quarter inch and a length of about an inch. Each of these pellets has a mass of only 8.5 grams, yet can produce as much energy as a ton of coal!

After the uranium has been formed into pellets, the pellets are stacked inside four-meter metal rods, which are then bound together to form fuel assemblies, which themselves are bound together inside the reactor core. The reactor core is a heavy steel container. Neutrons are then fired into the reactor core, where they dislodge neutrons from the unstable uranium atoms. Because the uranium is packed so tightly within the reactor core, any neutrons that are knocked loose from one atom go on to dislodge other neutrons from atoms, a chain reaction that enables the release of massive amounts of energy.

The core of a nuclear reactor gets extremely hot, so a coolant is used. Typically, this coolant is water, although breeder reactors, which get much hotter than conventional ones, use liquid sodium. In a breeder reactor, the fission of uranium produces plutonium, which itself can be used as nuclear fuel. The coolant in a nuclear reactor is also useful as a moderator, which means that it slows down the neutrons. This makes it easier to modulate the efficiency of the reactor's operation. Without coolant, the fuel rods in the reactor core may melt, at which point the control rods will not be able to control the reaction. The reactor core may become so hot that it triggers a meltdown, in which the floor beneath the reactor is disintegrated and radioactive material is released into the environment.

8. Which of the following would be the best title for this passage?
   a. "The Production of Nuclear Power"
   b. "Nuclear Waste Disposal"
   c. "The Uses of Uranium"
   d. "Reactors and Coolants"

9. Which of the following statements about the uranium used in nuclear power production is true?
     a. It does not need to be processed before use.
     b. It can be used to produce weapons.
     c. It cannot be purified.
     d. It occurs naturally.

10. Based on the information in the passage, seventeen grams of uranium fuel could produce as much energy as
     a. half a ton of coal.
     b. a ton of coal.
     c. two tons of coal.
     d. three tons of coal.

11. According to the passage, why does dislodging one neutron in the reactor core result in a chain reaction?
     a. Because the material is radioactive
     b. Because it is packed so tightly
     c. Because uranium is unstable
     d. Because the reactor must be cooled

12. Out of what metal is the reactor core constructed?
     a. iron
     b. steel
     c. uranium
     d. plutonium

13. What is the subject of the passage's final paragraph?
     a. the cooling of the reactor
     b. water
     c. how the reactor works
     d. nuclear meltdowns

14. What is the typical coolant in a nuclear reactor?
     a. water
     b. natural gas
     c. plutonium
     d. liquid sodium

Passage #3

Electricity is an essential part of modern life, but it can be dangerous and even deadly if proper safety procedures are not followed. When the amount of current passing through a wire increases, so does the amount of heat generated. If the wires become too hot, they can start a fire. Therefore, before electricity could be used within the home, there needed to be devices that could diminish, divert, or turn off electrical current. The three most common tools for this purpose are fuses, breakers, and switches.

There are two main types of fuse available for use in homes: the Edison-base fuse and the type S fuse. An Edison-base fuse screws into a socket by means of a threaded, spiraled bottom, much like a lightbulb. This is convenient, but it also makes it very easy to screw the wrong fuse into the socket. If an Edison-base fuse is screwed into a socket that requires a much higher voltage, it will blow immediately. If the fuse is screwed into a socket that requires much lower voltage, it will fail to blow even when dangerous levels of electricity are passing through the wire.

The potential for this error was eliminated with the introduction of the type S fuse, so called because the wire inside the fuse is bent into an S shape. The type S fuse is specially sized and designed so that fuses can only be screwed into the appropriate sockets. Still, fuses are considered too unreliable for use in the home and are used more often in cars these days.

In most homes, electrical safety is provided by a system of circuit breakers. Like a fuse, a circuit contains a bimetallic strip, through which the current passes. As the current increases, the strip begins to bend; if the current becomes too great, the strip will bend too much, and the circuit will be broken.

Of course, in order for a fuse or breaker to be effective, it must be at the right place in the circuit. For instance, many appliances contain a grounding wire, which connects the circuit with the casing (that is, the outside of the appliance). If a hot wire comes into contact with the casing, the current immediately blows the fuse or trips the breaker. In this arrangement, the switch, fuse, or circuit breaker must always be on the high-voltage, rather than the ground, side of the line. If the switch or fuse was placed on the ground side, an open circuit would have no current but would retain a potential current, which a person could complete, at his or her peril, by touching the appliance.

15. What would be the best title for this passage?
    a. "Edison-base fuses, type S fuses, circuit breakers, and grounding wires"
    b. "Electrical Safety Devices"
    c. "Deadly Electricity"
    d. "Switches, etc."

16. Which of the following is NOT one of the common devices for maintaining electrical safety?
    a. fuse
    b. battery
    c. switch
    d. breaker

17. What is the major problem with the Edison-base fuse?
    a. They are no longer manufactured
    b. They occasionally explode
    c. They are very expensive
    d. Every fuse fits into every socket

18. Why does the S type fuse have that name?
    a. Because the wire inside is shaped like an S
    b. Because it came after the R type fuse
    c. Because it requires S type batteries
    d. Because it screws into a socket

19. What does a grounding wire connect?
    a. the casing and the fuse
    b. the circuit and the casing
    c. the breaker and the circuit
    d. the fuse and the circuit

20. What is the purpose of an Edison-base fuse's threaded bottom?
    a. To combine with a grounding wire
    b. To indicate the appropriate level of current
    c. To improve the efficiency of the fuse
    d. To enable the fuse to be screwed into a socket

21. On an electrical appliance, where is the casing?
    a. On the outside
    b. Underneath
    c. Above
    d. Behind the electronic display

Passage #4

A modern steam power plant is fairly simple in its operation. In short, a coal fire turns water into steam inside a turbine, and the resulting pressure drives an alternator. The steam is then condensed back into water so that it can be used again. This process seems fairly simple, though in recent decades it has been modified slightly to improve the efficiency of these plants.

In a modern steam power plant, coal arrives by means of road, rail, or water. A series of fuel feeding devices transport the coal to the furnaces, where it is burnt. All of the ash that is produced by the burning of coal will be shunted to the back of the furnace and placed on scrap conveyors, which will then remove the ash to a storage compartment. Modern coal-fired steam power plants have electronic controls that govern the relative amounts of air and coal allowed into the furnace, which moderates the rate of combustion.

Meanwhile, a fan draws air from the outside into the plant, where it is preheated and then further warmed by the flue gases as they pass to the chimney. This air is then sent into the furnace. The preheating of the furnace air improves the efficiency of the plant considerably.

The heat from the furnace converts the water in the turbines to steam, which powers an alternator. After this steam leaves the turbine, it enters a condenser, so that it can be reconverted to water and used again. The modern steam power plant uses a condensate pump to remove the water from the condenser, at which point it enters a low-pressure water heater. This heater receives its warmth from the steam that escapes from the turbine. The water is further reheated in a high-pressure water heater, and then it is pumped into a boiler. Inside the boiler, the water is converted into high-pressure wet steam, where it is heated even further and fed into the turbine.

At the same time, the modern steam power plant will be circulating cool water throughout the facility, but especially around the condenser. This water will be drawn from a nearby natural source, such as a river or lake. The plant will need to use filters to prevent sediment and other particulate matter from damaging the machinery.

22. What affects the rate of combustion in the furnace?
    a. the amount of air only
    b. the amount of coal only
    c. both the amount of air and the amount of coal
    d. neither the amount of air nor the amount of coal

23. Which of the following would be the best title for this passage?
    a. "How a Modern Steam Power Plant Works"
    b. "The Operation of a Power Plant"
    c. "I Dream of Steam"
    d. "The Pros and Cons of Steam Power Plants"

24. In a modern steam power plant, water is pumped out of the condenser and into a
    a. furnace.
    b. high-pressure heater.
    c. low-pressure heater.
    d. turbine.

25. When the passage mentions in the second paragraph that ash will be "shunted," what is the closest synonym?
    a. moved
    b. destroyed
    c. burnt
    d. purchased

26. What is the main purpose of this passage?
    a. To advocate the construction of new steam power plants
    b. To describe how the primary energy source arrives at a steam power plant
    c. To entertain the reader with a story about steam power
    d. To explain the operation of a modern steam power plant

27. Why is cool water circulated around the condenser?
    a. So that the water can be reheated
    b. Because keeping the condenser cool helps it turn the steam back into water
    c. To prevent it from escaping the facility
    d. To power the condenser's operation

28. What is the primary subject of the last paragraph?
    a. the steam that spins the turbines
    b. the water used to cool the plant
    c. the employees of the plant
    d. the water used to spin the turbines

Passage #5

Despite its bad reputation in the United States, nuclear power has some advantages for the environment over other sources of energy. Oil, coal, and natural gas all release carbon dioxide and other gases that contribute to global warming, but nuclear power does not. Moreover, nuclear power plants generate neither sulfur oxides nor nitrogen oxides, so they do not contribute to acid rain.

However, nuclear plants do generate hazardous waste. The rods used for fuel expire and need to be replaced. These rods are extremely radioactive. Moreover, there are thousands of nuclear power plants around the world, so the total amount of high-level nuclear waste is significant. In some countries, such as France, the problem of disposing of this material is solved by reusing it. However, in the United States the breeder reactors that make reuse possible have not been viable at the commercial level, so safely disposing of nuclear waste continues to bedevil politicians, plant owners, and environmentalists.

At present, a number of approaches are used in the United States for the disposal of waste. In over thirty states, high-level nuclear waste is stored in above-ground facilities. However, some groups are beginning to use geologic repository systems, in which the waste is encased in lead or concrete and buried in an underground tunnel. This method of disposal is promising, but it is impossible in areas where earthquakes are likely or where groundwater can seep in.

Another possibility is called subductive waste disposal. This entails attaching or embedding hazardous waste to a tectonic plate that is in the process of sliding underneath another and would therefore carry the waste into the Earth's mantle. This inventive solution would most likely use the tectonic plates at the bottom of the ocean, both because these are out of the way and because they are the plates most actively engaged in subduction. However, the rate at which tectonic plates move is so slow (a few centimeters a year) that subductive waste disposal has largely been dismissed. Even its proponents admit that it would require storage techniques superior to those in use at present.

A final idea focuses on the disposal of weapons-grade plutonium. In what is known as the mixed oxide method, plutonium is mixed with uranium so that it can be used again in nuclear reactors. The waste that would result from this second round of power generation would be hazardous still, but less hazardous than the source plutonium. At the very least, the waste material derived from the mixed oxide method cannot be used in weaponry and is much easier to store.

29. The subject of this passage is
    a. subductive waste disposal.
    b. nuclear power plants.
    c. nuclear waste disposal.
    d. nuclear power.

30. Which of the following harmful gases is produced by nuclear power plants?
    a. carbon dioxide
    b. sulfur dioxide
    c. nitrogen dioxide
    d. None of the above

31. Which of the following sentences best asserts the main idea of the passage?
    a. "However, nuclear plants do generate hazardous waste."
    b. "Despite its bad reputation in the United States, nuclear power has some advantages for the environment over other sources of energy."
    c. "Oil, coal, and natural gas all release carbon dioxide and other gases that contribute to global warming, but nuclear power does not."
    d. "Moreover, there are thousands of nuclear power plants around the world, so the total amount of high-level nuclear waste is significant."

32. Which of the following statements about nuclear power in the United States is true?
    a. All of the nuclear waste in the United States is disposed of in the same way.
    b. There are a number of active breeder reactors in the United States.
    c. The United States employs several different methods for nuclear waste disposal.
    d. The United States is the only country to use subductive waste disposal techniques.

33. Which method of nuclear waste disposal involves creating a new form of nuclear fuel?
    a. mixed oxide
    b. subductive waste disposal
    c. hazardous waste sequestration
    d. geologic repository

34. When one tectonic plate slides underneath another, it is called
    a. repository.
    b. inferiority.
    c. sequestration.
    d. subduction.

35. What is the main problem with subductive waste disposal?
    a. Tectonic plates move too slowly.
    b. It requires plutonium to be converted into uranium.
    c. Subduction occurs too quickly.
    d. It is susceptible to contamination by groundwater.

36. Which of the following statements about the mixed oxide method is true?
    a. The resulting plutonium can be used in weapons.
    b. It produces waste that is easier to store.
    c. It involves mixing plutonium with thorium.
    d. It requires storage facilities under the sea.

Assembly

In this portion of the exam test takers need to figure out how an object would look after being properly assembled. The first picture in each problem displays all the parts that need to be assembled. The next five illustrations display five different methods of assembly, four of which are wrong, and one of which is right.

Every part has at least one letter marking it; some have more than one. Each letter represents a place on the assembled part. Some letters are also shown that correspond to unseen areas. These are displayed with a dotted line that points to the side underneath, or the unseen area.

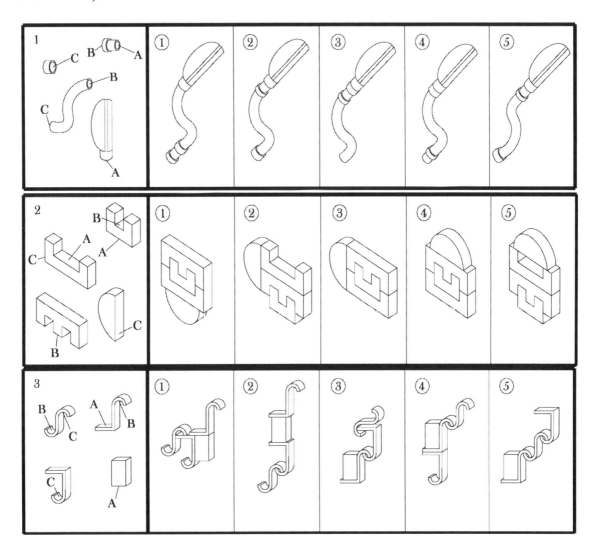

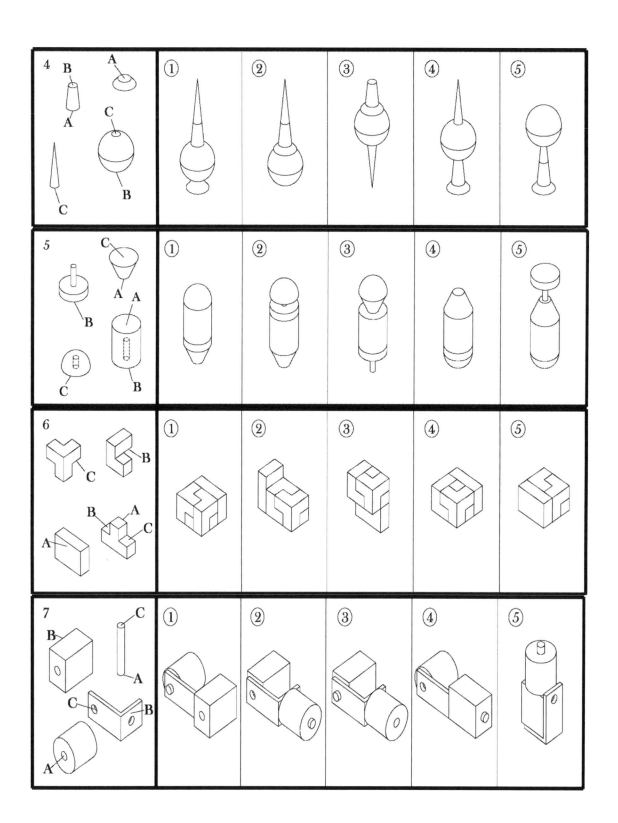

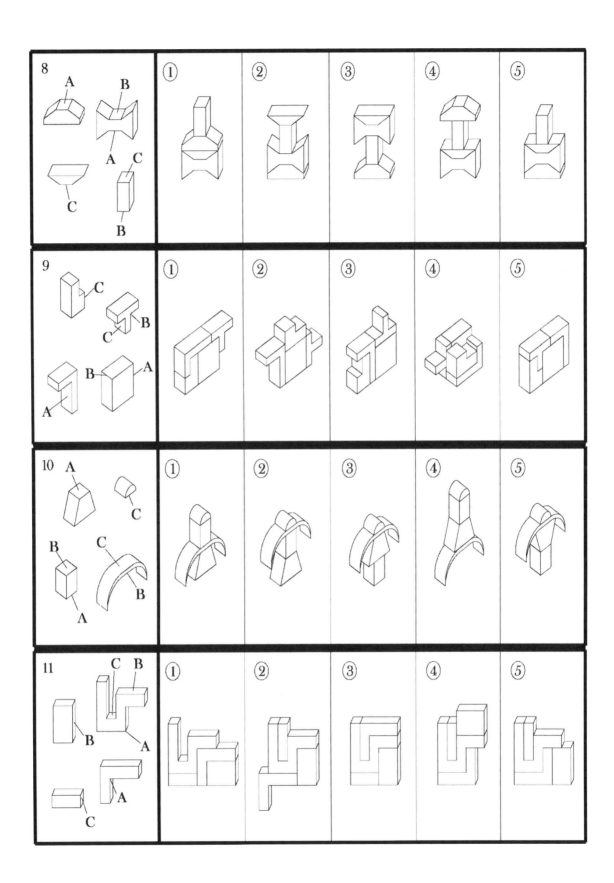

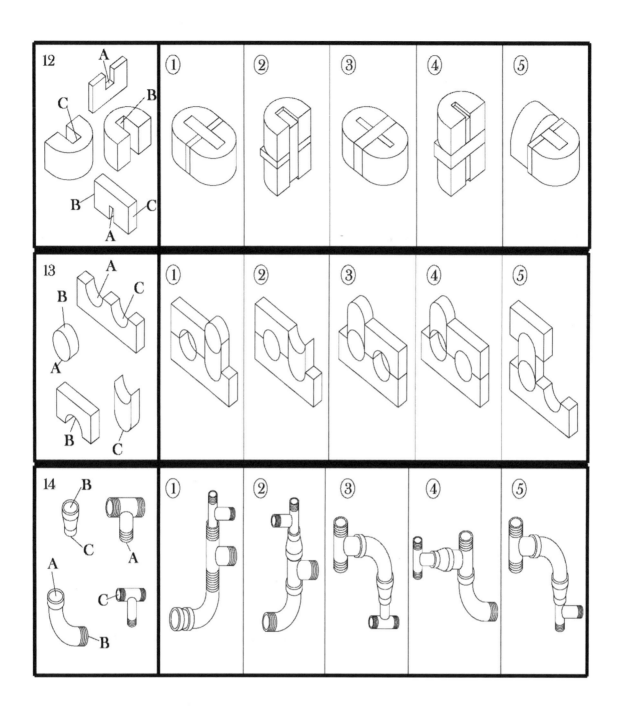

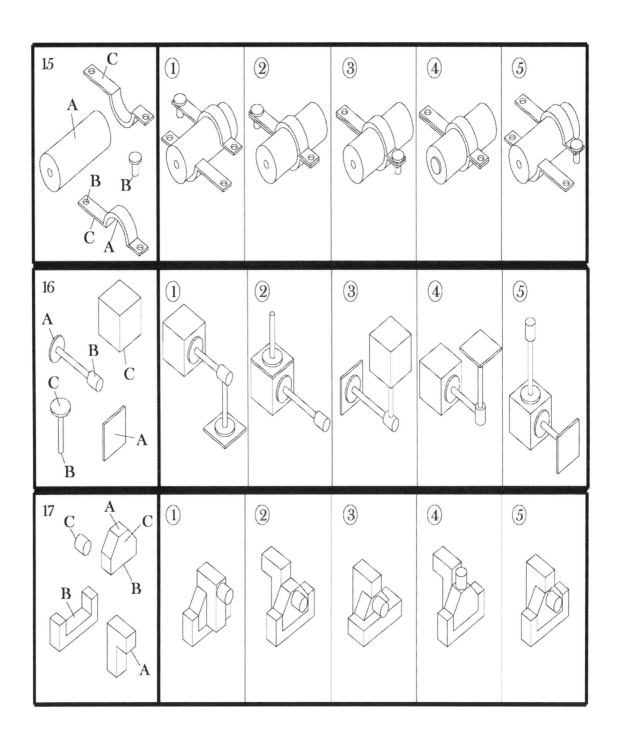

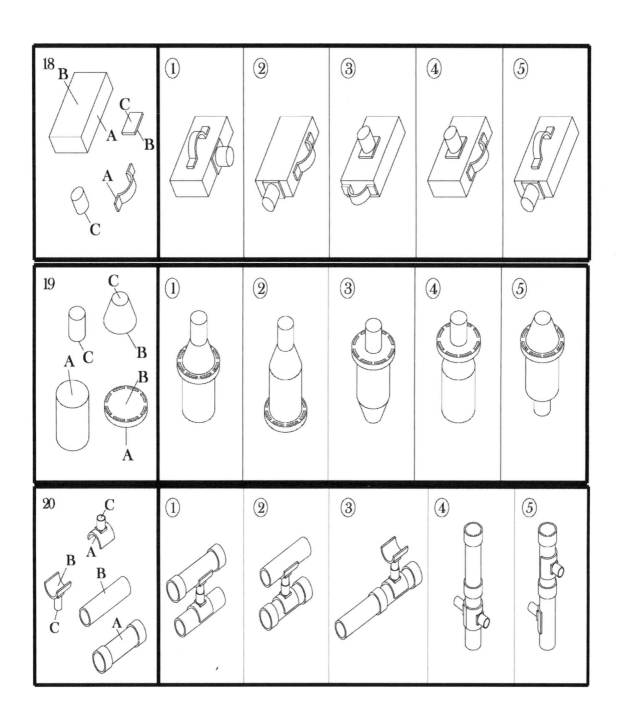

Mechanical Concepts

This is a test of your ability to understand mechanical concepts. Each question has a picture, a question and three possible answers. Read each question carefully, study the picture, and decide which answer is correct.

1. Objects 1 and 2 are submerged in separate tanks, both filled with water. In which tank (A or B) will the water level be the highest? (If equal, mark C)

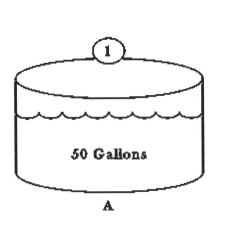
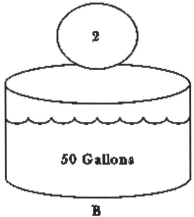

2. If ball 1 and ball 2 are of equal weight and moving at the same speed, in which direction (A, B or C) will ball 1 tend to go when it collides with ball 2 at point X?

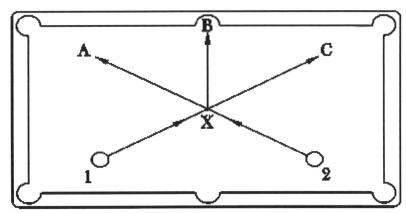

3. In which direction (A or B) will gear 5 spin if gear 1 is spinning counter-clockwise? (If both, mark C)

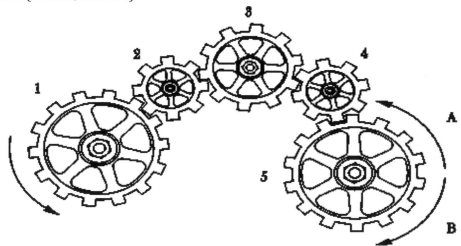

4. Which of the two identical objects (A or B) will launch a higher distance when the springs are released? (If equal, mark C)

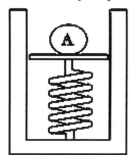

5. A watering can is filled with water. Which of the pictures (A or B) shows a more accurate representation of how the water will rest?

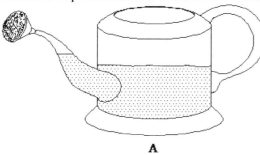
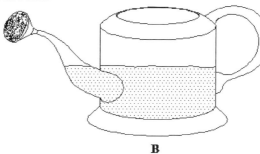

A

B

6. Among this arrangement of three pulleys, which pulley (A, B or C) turns fastest?

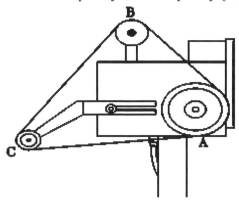

7. Which of the two scenarios (A or B) requires more effort to pull the weight up off the ground? (If equal, mark C)

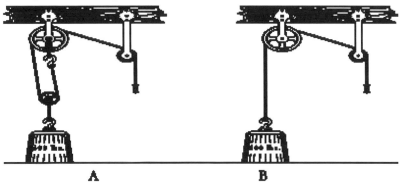

8. Which switch (A, B or C) should be closed in order to start the pump motor?

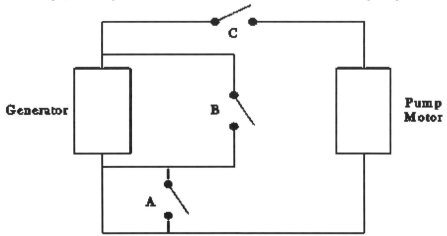

9. Which situation (A or B) requires more force to peddle the bicycle up the ramp? (If equal, mark C)

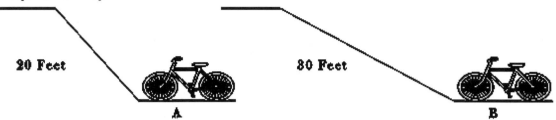

10. When the spring is released, the ball travels away from the spring to its highest point (A) and then begins to travel back towards its place of origin. At which point (A, B or C) will the ball travel to after it hits the spring a second time?

11. Which of the two boulders of equal weight (A or B) requires more force to push up the hill? (If equal, mark C)

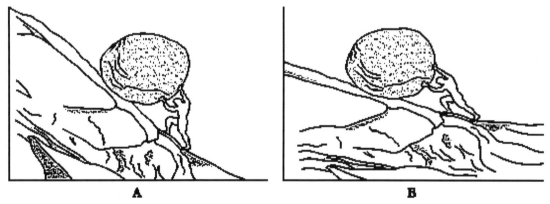

12. At which point (A, B or C) will the cannonball be traveling the slowest?

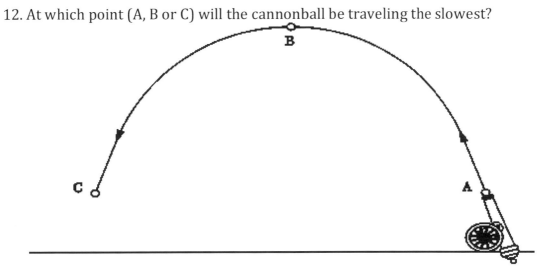

13. On which side of the pipe (A or B) would the water speed be slower? (If equal, mark C)

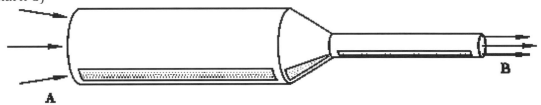

14. In which of the two figures (A or B) is the person bearing more weight? (If equal, mark C)

15. Which of the two lift trucks (A or B) carrying the same amount of weight is more likely to tip over? (If equal, mark C)

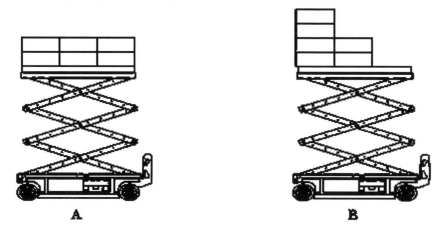

A   B

16. The weight of the boxes is being carried by the two men shown below. Which of the two men (A or B) is carrying more weight? (If equal, mark C)

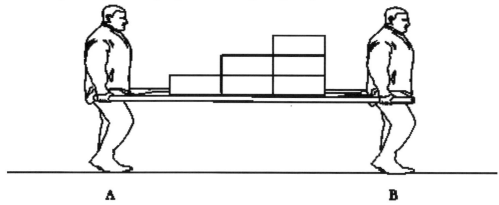

A   B

17. In the pictures below, which of the angles (A or B) is braced more solidly? (If equal, mark C)

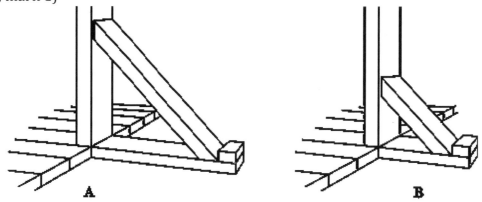

A   B

18. Given two birds sitting on branches of a tree at different elevations. Both drop objects of identical size and weight. Which object (A or B) will hit the ground with bigger force? (If equal, mark C)

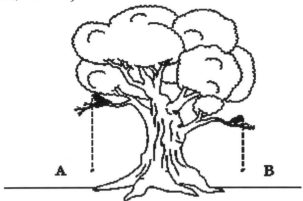

19. Which of the two wagons (A or B) of equal size and weight would be easier to drag up the hill? (If equal, mark C)

20. In which of the three positions (A, B or C) will it be easiest to accurately measure the amount of liquid in the graduated cylinder?

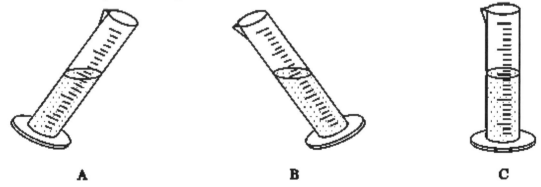

21. In which of the two figures (A or B) will the person require less force to lift a 100 pound weight? (If equal, mark C)

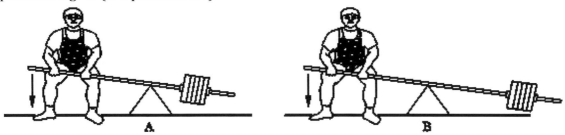

22. Which switch (A, B or C) should be closed to give power to the light?

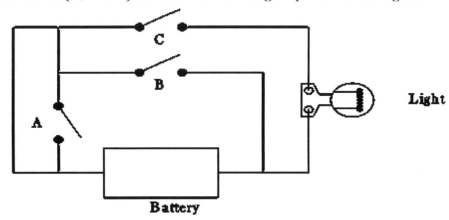

23. If the baseball and bowling ball are moving at the same speed, in which direction will the bowling ball tend to go when it collides with the baseball at point X?

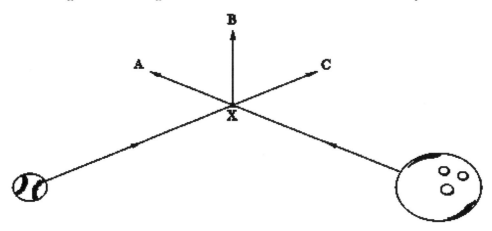

24. Which of the two rolls of paper towels (A or B) will undergo more revolutions if the ends of each roll were pulled downward with the same amount of force? (If equal, mark C)

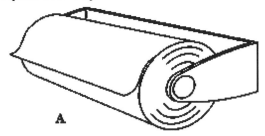
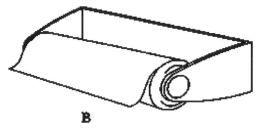

25. In which of the two containers (A or B) will water that is boiled to the same temperature cool more slowly? (If equal, mark C)

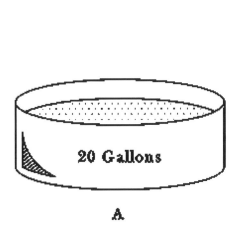
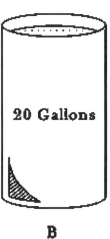

26. The water container A contains 50% salt. The water container B contains 25% salt. In which of the two containers (A or B) is an egg more likely to float? (If equal, mark C)

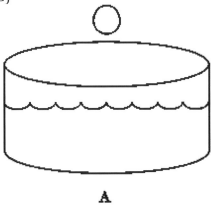
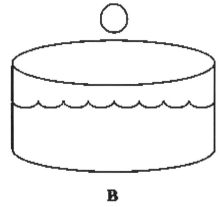

27. Which reflector (A or B) on the bicycle wheel is going to be traveling a greater distance when the wheel turns? (If equal, mark C)

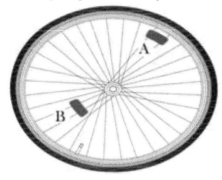

28. A javelin is thrown into the air. At which point (A, B or C) will the javelin be traveling the fastest?

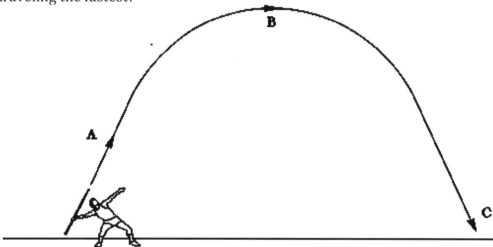

29. A child is released on the seat of a swing set at the position shown. To which point (A, B or C) will the child travel before he/she begins to return back to the point of origin?

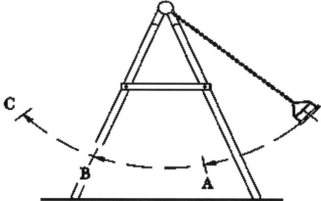

30. On which side of the pipe (A or B) would the water speed be slower? (If equal, mark C)

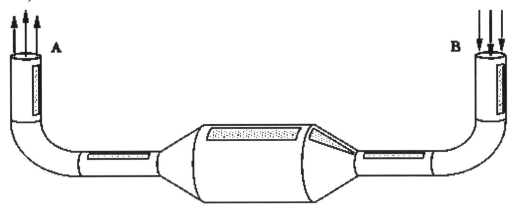

31. Given two objects shown below that are dropped from an elevation of 100 feet. Neglecting air resistance, which object (A or B) will fall at a faster rate? (If equal, mark C)

A   B

32. An athlete is holding a heavy metal ball attached to a wire and is rotating in the circular motion shown below. In which direction (A, B or C) would the ball travel when it is released at point X?

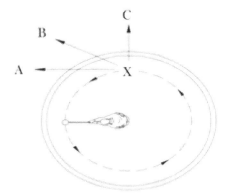

33. Which of the two wheels (A or B) will allow you to travel a further distance given the same rotational speed? (If equal, mark C)

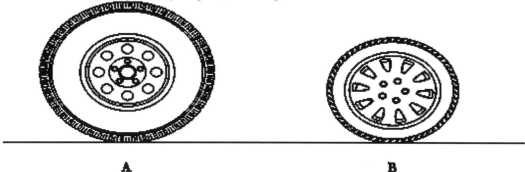

A   B

34. Two tanks with different capacities contain the same amount of gas, 50 kg. In which of the given tanks (A or B) will the gas pressure be greater? (If equal, mark C)

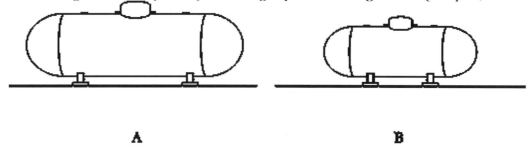

A   B

35. Given two water towers with identical tanks and identical amounts of water in each tank, which tower (A or B) will have greater water pressure coming out of the hose? (If equal, mark C)

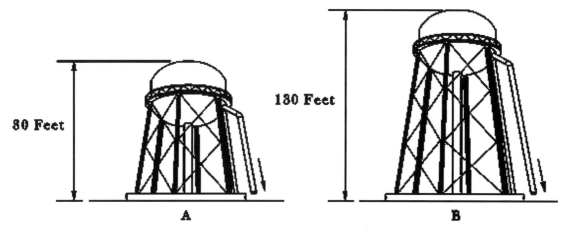

80 Feet   130 Feet

A   B

36. The weight of the boxes is resting on a platform suspended in the air by two ropes. Which of the two ropes (A or B) is supporting more of the weight? (If equal, mark C)

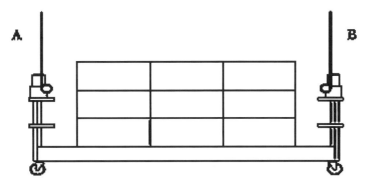

37. Container A contains 100 ml pure water and container B contains 100 ml vinegar. Assume an object is thrown into either container; in which of these two containers is the object more likely to float? (If equal, mark C)

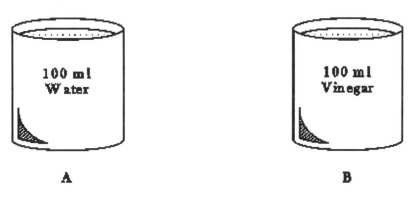

38. Which of the two scenarios (A or B) requires less effort to pull the weight up off the ground? (If equal, mark C)

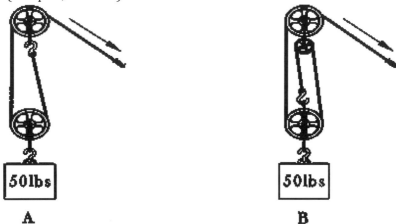

39. In which situation (A or B) will the ball reach the bottom of the ramp quicker? (If equal, mark C)

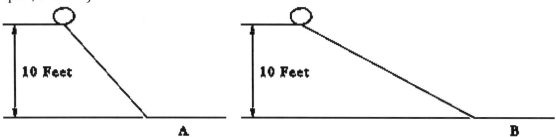

40. Container A holds 1 qt of water and container B holds 1 qt of motor oil. Assume each container is poured down a funnel at the same time. Which of the two contents will reach the bottom of the funnel more quickly? (If equal, mark C)

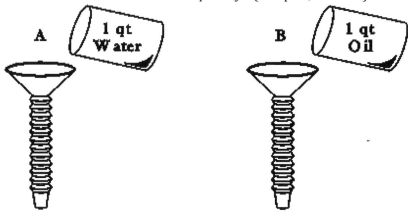

41. A full goblet is attached to the inside of a wheel rotating at a rate of 30 revolutions per second. In which direction (A or B) will the contents of the glass tend to go as the wheel rotates? (If none, mark C)

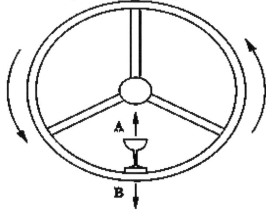

42. Which car (A or B) will travel a greater distance on the given track? (If equal, mark C)

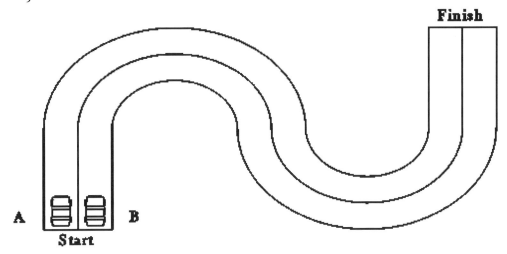

43. In which direction (A or B) will the ball move once the sticks of dynamite explode? (If neither, mark C)

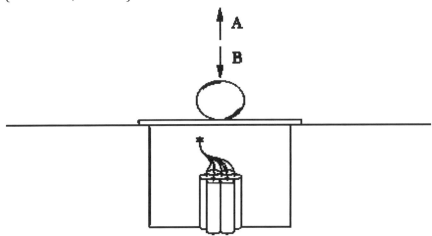

44. In which direction (A or B) will pulley 4 spin if pulley 1 is spinning counter-clockwise? (If none, mark C)

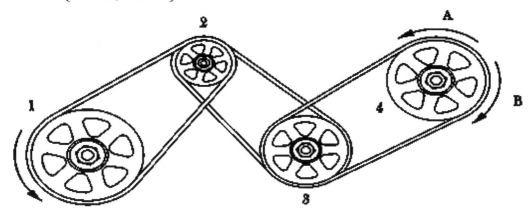

Tables and Graphs

The Tables and Graphs selection test measures speed and accuracy in reading tables and graphs. Part I contains a table of numbers, which is used to answer multiple-choice questions. Part II contains a graph which is used to answer multiple-choice questions.

Part I - Table

Cannonball horizontal distance traveled (m)							
Exit velocity m/s	**Barrel angle (degrees)**						
	15	**20**	**25**	**30**	**35**	**40**	**45**
10	5.102	6.559	7.817	8.837	9.589	10.049	10.204
20	20.408	26.236	31.267	35.348	38.355	40.196	40.816
30	45.918	59.032	70.351	79.533	86.298	90.442	91.837
40	81.633	104.945	125.068	141.392	153.419	160.785	163.265
50	127.551	163.976	195.420	220.925	239.718	251.226	255.102
60	183.673	236.126	281.404	318.132	345.193	361.766	367.347
70	250.000	321.394	383.022	433.013	469.846	492.404	500.000
80	326.531	419.780	500.274	565.568	613.677	643.140	653.061
90	413.265	531.284	633.159	715.797	776.685	813.974	826.531
100	510.204	655.906	781.678	883.699	958.870	1004.906	1020.408
110	617.347	793.646	945.830	1069.276	1160.233	1215.936	1234.694
120	734.694	944.504	1125.616	1272.527	1380.773	1447.064	1469.388
130	862.245	1108.481	1321.036	1493.452	1620.490	1698.291	1724.490
140	1000.000	1285.575	1532.089	1732.051	1879.385	1969.616	2000.000
150	1147.959	1475.788	1758.776	1988.324	2157.458	2261.038	2295.918

Part I Questions

	Exit Velocity m/s	Barrel Angle (degrees)	Cannonball Horizontal Distance Traveled (m)			
			A	B	C	D
1	100	30	958.870 O	883.699 O	715.797 O	781.678 O
2	10	45	40.816 O	10.049 O	10.204 O	40.196 O
3	90	20	531.284 O	413.265 O	633.159 O	419.780 O
4	110	15	793.646 O	510.204 O	617.347 O	734.694 O
5	130	35	1698.291 O	1493.452 O	1879.385 O	1620.490 O
6	50	40	239.718 O	251.226 O	255.102 O	361.766 O
7	30	25	70.351 O	59.032 O	79.533 O	31.267 O
8	140	45	2295.918 O	1969.616 O	2000.000 O	2261.038 O
9	40	20	125.068 O	104.945 O	81.633 O	163.976 O
10	20	30	38.355 O	31.267 O	79.533 O	35.348 O
11	150	35	2261.038 O	1879.385 O	2157.458 O	1988.324 O
12	60	15	183.673 O	127.551 O	163.976 O	236.126 O
13	120	40	1698.291 O	1469.388 O	1380.773 O	1447.064 O
14	60	25	236.126 O	281.404 O	220.925 O	383.022 O
15	10	20	5.102 O	9.589 O	6.559 O	10.049 O
16	130	30	1493.452 O	1321.036 O	1272.527 O	1620.490 O
17	130	15	734.694 O	862.245 O	944.504 O	1108.481 O
18	110	40	1234.694 O	1160.233 O	1020.408 O	1215.936 O
19	70	45	500.000 O	492.404 O	367.347 O	653.061 O
20	70	35	433.013 O	345.193 O	469.846 O	492.404 O
21	40	25	104.945 O	125.068 O	141.392 O	195.420 O
22	40	15	45.918 O	104.945 O	59.032 O	81.633 O
23	150	20	1475.788 O	1532.089 O	1758.776 O	1147.959 O
24	140	35	1732.051 O	1620.490 O	1969.616 O	1879.385 O
25	20	40	40.816 O	38.355 O	40.196 O	10.049 O
26	100	45	1234.694 O	1020.408 O	1215.936 O	1004.906 O
27	70	30	565.568 O	469.846 O	433.013 O	318.132 O
28	100	25	781.678 O	945.830 O	883.699 O	655.906 O
29	60	20	163.976 O	281.404 O	321.394 O	236.126 O
30	20	15	26.236 O	20.408 O	45.918 O	31.267 O

	Exit Velocity m/s	Barrel Angle (degrees)	Cannonball Horizontal Distance Traveled (m)			
			A	B	C	D
31	90	40	813.974 O	643.140 O	1004.906 O	826.531 O
32	140	25	1758.776 O	1321.036 O	1532.089 O	1493.452 O
33	80	30	715.797 O	565.568 O	433.013 O	500.274 O
34	100	35	1160.233 O	776.685 O	883.699 O	958.870 O
35	30	45	163.265 O	90.442 O	91.837 O	86.298 O
36	120	25	1125.616 O	1108.481 O	945.830 O	1272.527 O
37	110	20	944.504 O	945.830 O	793.646 O	655.906 O
38	10	40	10.204 O	10.049 O	40.196 O	9.589 O
39	50	30	239.718 O	195.420 O	153.419 O	220.925 O
40	60	35	239.718 O	469.846 O	345.193 O	433.013 O
41	70	25	383.022 O	321.394 O	500.274 O	281.404 O
42	80	15	413.265 O	326.531 O	321.394 O	531.284 O
43	40	45	160.785 O	255.102 O	251.226 O	163.265 O
44	150	25	1758.776 O	1732.051 O	1532.089 O	1475.788 O
45	10	30	9.589 O	7.817 O	8.837 O	6.559 O
46	30	35	153.419 O	86.298 O	79.533 O	90.442 O
47	30	40	91.837 O	86.298 O	160.785 O	90.442 O
48	50	20	163.976 O	195.420 O	236.126 O	104.945 O
49	90	25	781.678 O	500.274 O	633.159 O	565.568 O
50	130	25	1532.089 O	1321.036 O	1125.616 O	1493.452 O
51	80	20	500.274 O	419.780 O	413.265 O	326.531 O
52	60	40	492.404 O	251.226 O	367.347 O	361.766 O
53	120	30	1493.452 O	1380.773 O	1272.527 O	1125.616 O
54	80	35	613.677 O	776.685 O	715.797 O	469.846 O
55	90	30	776.685 O	715.797 O	565.568 O	883.699 O
56	50	35	239.718 O	220.925 O	251.226 O	345.193 O
57	140	20	1475.788 O	1108.481 O	1532.089 O	1285.575 O
58	140	30	1988.324 O	1493.452 O	1732.051 O	1879.385 O
59	110	45	1234.694 O	1469.388 O	1215.936 O	1020.408 O
60	120	35	1447.064 O	1380.773 O	1272.527 O	1215.936 O

Part II – Graph

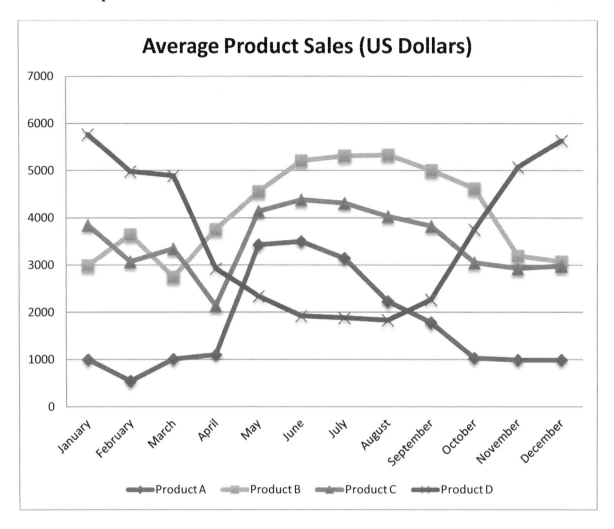

Part II Questions

	Month	Product Sales	Product A	Product B	Product C	Product D
1	May	4137.13	O	O	O	O
2	December	2978.31	O	O	O	O
3	January	996.32	O	O	O	O
4	April	2931.49	O	O	O	O
5	October	1032.11	O	O	O	O
6	September	3828.11	O	O	O	O
7	February	3074.56	O	O	O	O
8	August	2231.79	O	O	O	O
9	July	5311.22	O	O	O	O
10	December	5631.85	O	O	O	O
11	June	5207.18	O	O	O	O
12	March	1009.16	O	O	O	O
13	November	3198.87	O	O	O	O
14	May	2337.42	O	O	O	O
15	September	5002.62	O	O	O	O
16	March	3343.61	O	O	O	O
17	December	990.18	O	O	O	O
18	January	5772.34	O	O	O	O
19	February	3644.23	O	O	O	O
20	August	1834.66	O	O	O	O
21	May	3427.68	O	O	O	O
22	October	3754.61	O	O	O	O
23	July	4316.88	O	O	O	O
24	April	3751.97	O	O	O	O

Answers and Explanations

Mathematical Usage

1. D: 13.2 pounds

$$6 \; kilograms \; \times \frac{2.2 \; pounds}{1 \; kilogram} = 13.2 \; pounds$$

2. A: 160 rods

$$4 \; furlongs \times \frac{40 \; rods}{1 \; furlong} = 160 \; rods$$

3. A: 5 pounds

$$80 \; ounces \times \frac{1 \; pound}{16 \; ounces} = 5 \; pounds$$

4. C: 130,680 square feet

$$3 \; acres \times \frac{43,560 \; sq \; ft}{1 \; acre} = 130,680 \; sq \; ft$$

5. B: 3.218 kilometers

$$2 \; miles \times \frac{1.609 \; kilometers}{1 \; mile} = 3.218 \; kilometers$$

6. D: 0.75 gallons

$$3 \; quarts \; \times \frac{1 \; gallon}{4 \; quarts} = 0.75 \; gallons$$

7. C: 72 feet

$$12 \; fathoms \times \frac{6 \; feet}{1 \; fathom} = 72 \; feet$$

8. A: 3 barrels

$$126 \; gallons \times \frac{1 \; barrel}{42 \; gallons} = 3 \; barrels$$

9. D: 88 feet/sec

$$60 \frac{miles}{hr} \times \frac{4.4 \frac{feet}{sec}}{3 \frac{mile}{hr}} = 88 \frac{feet}{sec}$$

10. B: 0.5 kilograms

$$500 \ grams \times \frac{1 \ kilogram}{1000 \ grams} = 0.5 \ kilograms$$

11. D: 150 centimeters

$$15 \ hands \times \frac{10 \ centimeters}{1 \ hand} = 150 \ centimeters$$

12. C: 4 gallons

$$15.14 \ liters \times \frac{1 \ gallon}{3.785 \ liters} = 4 \ gallons$$

13. A: 336 quarts

$$2 \ barrels \times \frac{42 \ gallons}{1 \ barrel} \times \frac{4 \ quarts}{1 \ gallon} = 336 \ quarts$$

14. B: 160,934 centimeters

$$1 \ mile \times \frac{5280 \ feet}{1 \ mile} \times \frac{12 \ inches}{1 \ foot} \times \frac{2.54 \ centimeters}{1 \ inch} = 160,934 \ centimeters$$

Or, approximately:

$$1 \ mile \times \frac{1.609 \ kilometers}{1 \ mile} \times \frac{100,000 \ centimeters}{1 \ kilometer} = 160,900 \ centimeters$$

15. D: 6000 grams

$$13.2 \ pounds \times \frac{1 \ kilogram}{2.2 \ pounds} \times \frac{1000 \ grams}{1 \ kilogram} = 6000 \ grams$$

16. C: 576 inches

$$8 \ fathoms \times \frac{6 \ feet}{1 \ fathom} \times \frac{12 \ inches}{1 \ foot} = 576 \ inches$$

17. A: 7.57 liters

$$8 \ quarts \times \frac{1 \ gallon}{4 \ quarts} \times \frac{3.785 \ quarts}{1 \ gallon} = 7.57 \ liters$$

18. C: 152.4 centimeters

$$5 \ feet \times \frac{12 \ inches}{1 \ foot} \times \frac{2.54 \ centimeters}{1 \ inch} = 152.4 \ centimeters$$

19. C: Subtract 5 from both sides of the equation to get $8X = 56$. Divide both sides by 8 to get the answer, $X = 7$.

20. D: The least common denominator for the two fractions is 6, so multiply each term by 6 to get $2X = X + 24$. Subtract X from both sides to get $X = 24$.

21. B: Add 15 and $2X$ to both sides to get $5X = 15$. Divide both sides by 5 to get $X = 3$.

22. C: Since X is in the denominator, multiply each term by X to get $0.5 - 0.8X = 0.7$. Subtract 0.5 from both sides to get $-0.8X = 0.2$. Divide both sides by -0.8 to get -0.25.

23. D: Subtract 1.6 from both sides to get $0.4X = -0.6$. Divide both sides by 0.4 to get $X = -1.5$.

24. A: Subtract 0.5 from both sides to get $\frac{X}{0.4} = 2$. Multiply both sides by 0.4 to get $X = 0.8$.

25. B: Add 0.9 to both sides and subtract $0.5X$ from both sides to get $4.5X = 0.9$. Divide both sides by 4.5 to get $X = 0.2$.

26. C: Since X is in the denominator, multiply each term by X to get $1 - 0.2X = 0.3X$. Add $0.2X$ to both sides to get $1 = 0.5X$. Multiply both sides by 2 to get $X = 2$.

27. D: Subtract $0.4X$ from both sides to get $0.4X = 6$. Divide both sides by 0.4 to get $X = 15$.

28. B: Since X is in the denominator, multiply each term by X to get $2 = 1 + 2X$. Subtract 1 from both sides to get $1 = 2X$. Divide both sides by 2 to get $X = 0.5$.

29. E: Add $6X$ and 42 to both sides to get $7X = 42$. Divide both sides by 7 to get $X = 6$. Since this is not one of the choices listed, the answer is E, none of the above.

30. D: Since X is in the denominator, multiply each term by X to get $4 - 6X = -0.2$. Add $6X$ and 0.2 to both sides to get $4.2 = 6X$. Divide both sides by 6 to get $X = 0.7$.

31. A: Subtract 5 from both sides to get $2X = 6$. Divide both sides by 2 to get $X = 3$.

32. B: Add 4 to both sides to get $\frac{X}{0.2} = 20$. Multiply both sides by 0.2 to get $X = 4$.

33. B: The length of the fence will be the circumference of the circle it makes. The circumference is 2 × radius × π = 2 × 10 × 3.14 = 62.8 meters.

34. C: To convert Celsius to Fahrenheit, multiply the temperature by 1.8 and add 32. 45 × 1.8 + 32 = 113 °F

35. C: The volume of a cylinder is calculated by multiplying the base area by the height. The base of a cylinder is a circle, so to find the area of the base, use the circle

area formula. Base area = π × 30² = 2827.4 ft². Multiply this area by the height to find the volume: 2827.4 × 150 = 424,115 ft³.

36. D: Each wall is a rectangle measuring 9 ft by 20 ft, so the area of each wall is 9 × 20 = 180 ft². Since there are 4 walls, multiply 180 ft² by 4 to get 720 ft². Each can of paint can cover 120 ft², so divide the surface area by 120 to get 720/120 = 6 cans of paint.

37. D: The area of a rectangle is found by multiplying the length and width. Here, the area is given and the question requires you to find the length. Area = length × width, so 250,000 = length × 400. To find the length, divide the area by the known side length: 250,000/400 = 625 ft.

38. A: To convert Celsius to Kelvin, simply add 273.15. -80 + 273.15 = 193.15 K

39. B: Since the volume is staying the same, calculate the current volume, 2 × 10 × 18 = 360 in³. To find the unknown new height, divide the volume by the known new dimensions, 360/(2.5 × 12) = 360/30 = 12 inches.

40. A: The formula for the volume of a pyramid is (base area × height)/3. For a square base, this formula becomes [(side length)² × height]/3. Plugging in the numbers from the questions gives us [(side length)² × 160]/3 = 4,800,000. Multiply by 3 and divide by 160 to get s² = 10,000. Take the square root of both sides to find the side length = 100 ft.

41. B: To solve this problem, you have to convert temperature twice. First, Fahrenheit to Celsius. °C = (250 – 32)/1.8 = 121.11 °C. From Celsius, you can convert directly to Kelvin. K = 121.11 + 273.15 = 394.26 K.

42. A: First, calculate the area of the rectangular field, 10,000 × 2500 = 25,000,000 ft². Next find the size of the square that has that same area, s² = 25,000,000, s = 5,000 ft. So each side of the new field will be 5000 ft. Since all four sides of a square are the same, the perimeter will be 4 × 5000 = 20,000 ft.

43. A: Density is calculated by dividing the mass by the volume. The mass of the marble is given in the question as 50 g. The volume can be calculated using the formula for the volume of a sphere. Volume = (4/3) × (3.14) × 1³ = 4.189 cm³. Divide the mass of 50 g by the volume of 4.189 cm³: 50/4.189 = 11.94 g/cm³.

44. D: Degrees Rankine is calculated from degrees Fahrenheit by simply adding 459.67. Thus, the autoignition temperature in degrees Rankine is 685 + 459.67 = 1144.67 °R.

45. D: The formula for the volume of a cone is (base area × height)/3. The base area is the area of a circle, so the formula can be rewritten as [(π × radius²) × height]/3.

Plugging in the numbers gives [(3.14 × r²) × 60]/3 = 90,000. Multiply by 3, divide by 45, and divide by 3.14 to get r² = 1433 cm². Take the square root to find that r = 37.86 cm. However, we were asked for the diameter of the cone, so multiply the radius by 2 to find the diameter = 75.7 cm.

46. C: Although density is mentioned in the question, there is no need to use the density formula on this problem. Because the density is constant, the volume and mass are directly proportional, which means that if the volume increases by a factor of 2, so does the mass. To solve the problem, you just have to determine by what factor the volume increases. In the sphere volume formula, the radius is raised to the third power, which means that, whatever factor the radii differ by, the volumes will differ by that factor raised to the third power. Since the larger tank has 2 times the radius of the smaller tank, this means that the larger tank will have $2^3 = 8$ times the volume. Since volume and mass are directly proportional, the larger tank will hold 8 times as much mass or 8 × 10,000 = 80,000 kg.

Reading for Comprehension

1. A: This information is supplied in the last sentence of the first paragraph.

2. B: This is stated in the last sentence of the first paragraph.

3. D: The second sentence of the third paragraph states that hydroelectric power plants "cost a great deal of money to construct."

4. B: This sentence means that when hydroelectric power plants are compared with other power plants, the hydroelectric plants are found to have many superior qualities.

5. D: This can be inferred from the last sentence of the second paragraph, where it states that "hydroelectric plants are considered to be one of the most durable systems, which means that they maintain their efficiency throughout their lives."

6. B: The third sentence of the last paragraph states that, if the land is rocky, this "will make it better able to support the heavy equipment that must be used in construction and operation."

7. A: The last paragraph of the passage deals primarily with the selection of a site for a hydroelectric power plant, as indicated by the first sentence: "Clearly, hydroelectric power plants cannot be built just anywhere."

8. A: The passage is a general description of the operations in a nuclear reactor, ranging from the required fuel to the use of coolant.

9. D: This information is given in the second sentence of the second paragraph.

10. C: The second paragraph describes the uranium used to fuel a nuclear reactor and then mentions that, "Each of these [uranium] pellets has a mass of only 8.5 grams, yet can produce as much energy as a ton of coal!" Therefore, twice this amount of uranium should produce as much energy as two tons of coal.

11. B: In the fourth sentence of the third paragraph, it states that, "Because the uranium is packed so tightly within the reactor core, any neutrons that are knocked loose from one atom go on to dislodge other neutrons from atoms."

12. B: This information is given in the second sentence of the third paragraph.

13. A: The final paragraph discusses the need for coolant, the types of coolant used, and the catastrophic consequences of a lack of coolant.

14. A: This information is given in the second sentence of the last paragraph.

15. B: The passage discusses the various pieces of equipment used to make electricity safe.

16. B: The opening paragraph describes the importance of electrical safety and then, in the final sentence, states that "The three most common tools for this purpose are fuses, breakers, and switches."

17. D: The third sentence of the second paragraph refers to this problem, mentioning that it "makes it very easy to screw the wrong fuse into the socket." The rest of the second paragraph describes why this can be a dangerous mistake.

18. A: This is indicated in the first sentence of the third paragraph, which states that "so called because the wire inside the fuse is bent into an S shape."

19. B: The second sentence of the last paragraph states that a grounding wire "connects the circuit with the casing."

20. D: In the second sentence of the second paragraph, the passage states that "An Edison-base fuse screws into a socket by means of a threaded, spiraled bottom."

21. A: Within the parentheses in the second sentence of the last paragraph, the passage defines the casing as "the outside of the appliance."

22. C: This information is in the last sentence of the second paragraph.

23. A: The best title for this passage would be "How a Modern Steam Power Plant Works." The passage is entirely about the steps in the operation of a modern steam power plant. The answer choice "The Operation of a Power Plant," is not bad, but it is not as good as the correct choice because it does not identify the specific type of power plant discussed in the passage.

24. C: This information is in the third sentence of the fourth paragraph.

25. A: The passage says that ash is "shunted to the back of the furnace," meaning that it is moved there.

26. D: This is clear from the first sentence of the passage, "A modern steam power plant is fairly simple in its operation."

27. B: The first sentence of the last paragraph mentions that cool water is circulated "throughout the facility, but especially around the condenser." The second sentence of the fourth paragraph describes how a steam power plant uses condensers to turn steam back into water.

28. B: The last paragraph discusses how cool water is circulated through a steam power plant to cool the equipment, in particular the condenser.

29. C: The passage begins by describing the origins of nuclear waste and then details some possible solutions to this problem.

30. D: This information is given in the second and third sentences of the third paragraph.

31. A: The focus of the article is nuclear waste and its disposal.

32. C: This is stated in the first sentence of the third paragraph.

33. A: The final paragraph describes the mixed-oxide method, in which weapons-grade plutonium is mixed with uranium.

34. D: Subduction is never directly defined, but its meaning may be inferred from the context of the fourth paragraph.

35. A: The fourth paragraph of this passage describes subductive waste disposal. In the second-to-last sentence, it states that "the rate at which tectonic plates move is so slow (a few centimeters a year) that subductive waste disposal has largely been dismissed."

36. B: The mixed oxide method is discussed in the final paragraph of the passage.

Mechanical Concepts

1. B: Object 2 is larger than object 1, so it will displace more water and cause the water level in tank B to be higher than that of tank A.

2. A: Since momentum is conserved in all collisions, and there is no indication that the balls merge into one upon colliding, ball 1 must rebound off ball 2 toward the upper left pocket.

3. A: Consecutive gears alternate rotation direction, which means all odd numbered gears turn the same direction. Since 1 and 5 are both odd, both are spinning counter-clockwise in this problem.

4. B: The spring being compressed under object B is being compressed further, and therefore has more potential energy stored up to launch the ball higher into the air.

5. B: Water (along with nearly every other substance) seeks the lowest energy state in which to rest. Functionally, this means that the water level will be equally high in all parts of the watering can.

6. C: Every point on the belt, and consequently every point on the outside of each pulley, is moving at the same linear speed. Therefore, the pulley with the smallest circumference will rotate the fastest.

7. B: A pulley only reduces the amount of force required to lift an object if the weight is distributed across multiple sections of the rope, as is done in A.

8. C: Only switch C creates a closed loop between the generator and the motor. Closing B creates a short circuit, and closing A does nothing.

9. A: More force is required to propel a bicycle up a steeper slope.

10. B: Because of friction losses within the spring and between the ball and the surface, the ball will not travel as far the second time.

11. A: More force is required to push a boulder up a steeper slope.

12. B: In ballistic flight, the horizontal component of velocity is essentially constant. At point B, the vertical component of the cannonball's velocity is zero, making the peak of its arc the slowest point.

13. A: Since all the water must leave at the same rate at which it enters, the water must travel significantly faster at point B, since the opening is much smaller.

14. A: In figure A, the load is centered much closer to the man and much farther from the wheel than in figure B. This means that the man will have to bear a larger percentage of the weight of the load.

15. B: On truck A, the load is evenly distributed, while on truck B it is concentrated on one end, making it more likely to tip over.

16. B: The load on the stretcher is concentrated more closely to man B than man A, so man B is bearing more of the load.

17. A: The bracing in A is more solid because it extends higher up on the post.

18. A: Though the force of gravity is the same on both objects, object A will have had more time to build up speed, so it will hit the ground with more force than object B.

19. B: The wagon will roll more easily up the smoother slope.

20. C: The amount of liquid will be easiest to measure when the angle of the water line matches the lines drawn on the cylinder.

21. A: In figure A, the weight is much closer to the fulcrum, so it will require less force to raise.

22. C: Only switch C creates a closed loop between the battery and the light. Closing B creates a short circuit, and closing A does nothing.

23. A: Since a bowling ball weighs nearly 50 times as much as a baseball, the bowling ball's path will not be significantly affected by its collision with the baseball.

24. B: Roll B will turn faster, both because it is lighter, thus having a lower moment of inertia, and because it requires less paper to be pulled to undergo a revolution.

25. B: Water in container B will cool more slowly because less of the surface of the water is exposed to the air.

26. A: Adding salt to water increases the density of the fluid, making objects more likely to float in it.

27. A: Reflector A is farther from the center of the wheel. Therefore, it will travel more distance when the wheel turns.

28. C: Since air resistance on a javelin is negligible, and its horizontal velocity is effectively constant throughout its flight, the fastest point will be the point that has the greatest vertical velocity. Since point C is the lowest point, it is the point at which the maximum potential energy will have been converted to kinetic energy.

29. C: The child will travel to the approximately equivalent height on the other side of the swing set before returning to the initial side.

30. C: Since all the water must leave at the same rate at which it enters, and since both the entry and exit pipes have the same size, the water must be traveling at the same speed in both locations.

31. C: In the absence of air resistance, the acceleration of an object in freefall is independent of the object's size, shape, or mass. Thus, both objects will fall at the same rate.

32. A: When the ball is released, it will continue traveling in whatever linear direction it was traveling at the time of release. The path it takes will be along a line that is tangent to the circle.

33. A: Since wheel A is larger, it travels farther on each full rotation.

34. B: The same amount of gas will be under greater pressure in the smaller tank since there is less space for it to occupy.

35. B: Tank B is 50 feet higher than tank A, which means that the water it holds has an additional 50 feet of potential energy contributing to the pressure at the end of the hose.

36. C: Since the boxes are evenly distributed and their center is equal distance from both ropes, the two ropes support equal amounts of the weight.

37. C: Water and vinegar have essentially the same density, so an object will be no more likely to float in one than the other.

38. B: In figure A, the weight is split between two sections of the rope, while in figure B, it is distributed among three sections. This means that it will only require a third of the effort to lift the weight in figure B, versus half the weight in figure A.

39. A: The ball will accelerate down the steeper slope faster and reach the bottom more quickly.

40. A: Oil is much more viscous than water, so it will take longer to reach the bottom of the funnel.

41. C: Since the wheel is rotating so quickly, the contents of the goblet will remain in the place because of inertia.

42. C: Both paths are the same length. The first half of path A is identical to the second half of path B, and vice versa.

43. A: The force of the explosion will propel everything above it into the air.

44. A: Because these pulleys are connected by belts, they will all turn in the same direction.

Assembly, Tables, and Graphs

Assembly		Table				Graph	
Question	Answer	Question	Answer	Question	Answer	Question	Answer
1.	2	1.	B	31.	A	1.	C
2.	3	2.	C	32.	C	2.	C
3.	5	3.	A	33.	B	3.	A
4.	4	4.	C	34.	D	4.	D
5.	3	5.	D	35.	C	5.	A
6.	4	6.	B	36.	A	6.	C
7.	1	7.	A	37.	C	7.	C
8.	2	8.	C	38.	B	8.	A
9.	5	9.	B	39.	D	9.	B
10.	2	10.	D	40.	C	10.	D
11.	4	11.	C	41.	A	11.	B
12.	1	12.	A	42.	B	12.	A
13.	2	13.	D	43.	D	13.	B
14.	5	14.	B	44.	A	14.	D
15.	2	15.	C	45.	C	15.	B
16.	3	16.	A	46.	B	16.	C
17.	5	17.	B	47.	D	17.	A
18.	4	18.	D	48.	A	18.	D
19.	1	19.	A	49.	C	19.	B
20.	2	20.	C	50.	B	20.	D
		21.	B	51.	B	21.	A
		22.	D	52.	D	22.	D
		23.	A	53.	C	23.	C
		24.	D	54.	A	24.	B
		25.	C	55.	B		
		26.	B	56.	A		
		27.	C	57.	D		
		28.	A	58.	C		
		29.	D	59.	A		
		30.	B	60.	B		

Secret Key #1 - Time is Your Greatest Enemy

Pace Yourself

Wear a watch. At the beginning of the test, check the time (or start a chronometer on your watch to count the minutes), and check the time after every few questions to make sure you are "on schedule."

If you are forced to speed up, do it efficiently. Usually one or more answer choices can be eliminated without too much difficulty. Above all, don't panic. Don't speed up and just begin guessing at random choices. By pacing yourself, and continually monitoring your progress against your watch, you will always know exactly how far ahead or behind you are with your available time. If you find that you are one minute behind on the test, don't skip one question without spending any time on it, just to catch back up. Take 15 fewer seconds on the next four questions, and after four questions you'll have caught back up. Once you catch back up, you can continue working each problem at your normal pace.

Furthermore, don't dwell on the problems that you were rushed on. If a problem was taking up too much time and you made a hurried guess, it must be difficult. The difficult questions are the ones you are most likely to miss anyway, so it isn't a big loss. It is better to end with more time than you need than to run out of time.

Lastly, sometimes it is beneficial to slow down if you are constantly getting ahead of time. You are always more likely to catch a careless mistake by working more slowly than quickly, and among very high-scoring test takers (those who are likely to have lots of time left over), careless errors affect the score more than mastery of material.

Secret Key #2 - Practice Smarter, Not Harder

Many test takers delay the test preparation process because they dread the awful amounts of practice time they think necessary to succeed on the test. We have refined an effective method that will take you only a fraction of the time.

There are a number of "obstacles" in your way to succeed. Among these are answering questions, finishing in time, and mastering test-taking strategies. All must be executed on the day of the test at peak performance, or your score will suffer. The test is a mental marathon that has a large impact on your future.

Just like a marathon runner, it is important to work your way up to the full challenge. So first you just worry about questions, and then time, and finally strategy:

Success Strategy

1. Find a good source for practice tests.
2. If you are willing to make a larger time investment, consider using more than one study guide- often the different approaches of multiple authors will help you "get" difficult concepts.
3. Take a practice test with no time constraints, with all study helps "open book." Take your time with questions and focus on applying strategies.
4. Take a practice test with time constraints, with all guides "open book."
5. Take a final practice test with no open material and time limits

If you have time to take more practice tests, just repeat step 5. By gradually exposing yourself to the full rigors of the test environment, you will condition your mind to the stress of test day and maximize your success.

Secret Key #3 - Prepare, Don't Procrastinate

Let me state an obvious fact: if you take the test three times, you will get three different scores. This is due to the way you feel on test day, the level of preparedness you have, and, despite the test writers' claims to the contrary, some tests WILL be easier for you than others.

Since your future depends so much on your score, you should maximize your chances of success. In order to maximize the likelihood of success, you've got to prepare in advance. This means taking practice tests and spending time learning the information and test taking strategies you will need to succeed.

Never take the test as a "practice" test, expecting that you can just take it again if you need to. Feel free to take sample tests on your own, but when you go to take the official test, be prepared, be focused, and do your best the first time!

Secret Key #4 - Test Yourself

Everyone knows that time is money. There is no need to spend too much of your time or too little of your time preparing for the test. You should only spend as much of your precious time preparing as is necessary for you to get the score you need.

Once you have taken a practice test under real conditions of time constraints, then you will know if you are ready for the test or not.

If you have scored extremely high the first time that you take the practice test, then there is not much point in spending countless hours studying. You are already there.

Benchmark your abilities by retaking practice tests and seeing how much you have improved. Once you score high enough to guarantee success, then you are ready. If you have scored well below where you need, then knuckle down and begin studying in earnest. Check your improvement regularly through the use of practice tests under real conditions. Above all, don't worry, panic, or give up. The key is perseverance!

Then, when you go to take the test, remain confident and remember how well you did on the practice tests. If you can score high enough on a practice test, then you can do the same on the real thing.

General Strategies

The most important thing you can do is to ignore your fears and jump into the test immediately- do not be overwhelmed by any strange-sounding terms. You have to jump into the test like jumping into a pool- all at once is the easiest way.

Make Predictions

As you read and understand the question, try to guess what the answer will be. Remember that several of the answer choices are wrong, and once you begin reading them, your mind will immediately become cluttered with answer choices designed to throw you off. Your mind is typically the most focused immediately after you have read the question and digested its contents. If you can, try to predict what the correct answer will be. You may be surprised at what you can predict.

Quickly scan the choices and see if your prediction is in the listed answer choices. If it is, then you can be quite confident that you have the right answer. It still won't hurt to check the other answer choices, but most of the time, you've got it!

Answer the Question

It may seem obvious to only pick answer choices that answer the question, but the test writers can create some excellent answer choices that are wrong. Don't pick an answer just because it sounds right, or you believe it to be true. It MUST answer the question. Once you've made your selection, always go back and check it against the question and make sure that you didn't misread the question, and the answer choice does answer the question posed.

Benchmark

After you read the first answer choice, decide if you think it sounds correct or not. If it doesn't, move on to the next answer choice. If it does, mentally mark that answer choice. This doesn't mean that you've definitely selected it as your answer choice, it just means that it's the best you've seen thus far. Go ahead and read the next choice. If the next choice is worse than the one you've already selected, keep going to the next answer choice. If the next choice is better than the choice you've already selected, mentally mark the new answer choice as your best guess.

The first answer choice that you select becomes your standard. Every other answer choice must be benchmarked against that standard. That choice is correct until proven otherwise by another answer choice beating it out. Once you've decided that no other answer choice seems as good, do one final check to ensure that your answer choice answers the question posed.

Valid Information

Don't discount any of the information provided in the question. Every piece of information may be necessary to determine the correct answer. None of the information in the question is there to throw you off (while the answer choices will certainly have information to throw you off). If two seemingly unrelated topics are discussed, don't ignore either. You can be confident there is a relationship, or it wouldn't be included in the question, and you are probably going to have to determine what is that relationship to find the answer.

Avoid "Fact Traps"

Don't get distracted by a choice that is factually true. Your search is for the answer that answers the question. Stay focused and don't fall for an answer that is true but incorrect. Always go back to the question and make sure you're choosing an answer that actually answers the question and is not just a true statement. An answer can be factually correct, but it MUST answer the question asked. Additionally, two answers can both be seemingly correct, so be sure to read all of the answer choices, and make sure that you get the one that BEST answers the question.

Milk the Question

Some of the questions may throw you completely off. They might deal with a subject you have not been exposed to, or one that you haven't reviewed in years. While your lack of knowledge about the subject will be a hindrance, the question itself can give you many clues that will help you find the correct answer. Read the question carefully and look for clues. Watch particularly for adjectives and nouns describing difficult terms or words that you don't recognize. Regardless of if you completely understand a word or not, replacing it with a synonym either provided or one you more familiar with may help you to understand what the questions are asking. Rather than wracking your mind about specific detailed information concerning a difficult term or word, try to use mental substitutes that are easier to understand.

The Trap of Familiarity

Don't just choose a word because you recognize it. On difficult questions, you may not recognize a number of words in the answer choices. The test writers don't put "make-believe" words on the test; so don't think that just because you only recognize all the words in one answer choice means that answer choice must be correct. If you only recognize words in one answer choice, then focus on that one. Is it correct? Try your best to determine if it is correct. If it is, that is great, but if it doesn't, eliminate it. Each word and answer choice you eliminate increases your chances of getting the question correct, even if you then have to guess among the unfamiliar choices.

Eliminate Answers

Eliminate choices as soon as you realize they are wrong. But be careful! Make sure you consider all of the possible answer choices. Just because one appears right, doesn't mean that the next one won't be even better! The test writers will usually put more than one good answer choice for every question, so read all of them. Don't worry if you are stuck between two that seem right. By getting down to just two remaining possible choices, your odds are now 50/50. Rather than wasting too much time, play the odds. You are guessing, but guessing wisely, because you've been able to knock out some of the answer choices that you know are wrong. If you are eliminating choices and realize that the last answer choice you are left with is also obviously wrong, don't panic. Start over and consider each choice again. There may easily be something that you missed the first time and will realize on the second pass.

Tough Questions

If you are stumped on a problem or it appears too hard or too difficult, don't waste time. Move on! Remember though, if you can quickly check for obviously incorrect answer choices, your chances of guessing correctly are greatly improved. Before you completely give up, at least try to knock out a couple of possible answers. Eliminate what you can and then guess at the remaining answer choices before moving on.

Brainstorm

If you get stuck on a difficult question, spend a few seconds quickly brainstorming. Run through the complete list of possible answer choices. Look at each choice and ask yourself, "Could this answer the question satisfactorily?" Go through each answer choice and consider it independently of the other. By systematically going through all possibilities, you may find something that you would otherwise overlook. Remember that when you get stuck, it's important to try to keep moving.

Read Carefully

Understand the problem. Read the question and answer choices carefully. Don't miss the question because you misread the terms. You have plenty of time to read each question thoroughly and make sure you understand what is being asked. Yet a happy medium must be attained, so don't waste too much time. You must read carefully, but efficiently.

Face Value

When in doubt, use common sense. Always accept the situation in the problem at face value. Don't read too much into it. These problems will not require you to make huge leaps of logic. The test writers aren't trying to throw you off with a cheap trick. If you have to go beyond creativity and make a leap of logic in order to have an answer choice answer the question, then you should look at the other answer choices. Don't overcomplicate the problem by creating theoretical relationships or explanations that will warp time or space. These are normal problems rooted in reality. It's just that the applicable relationship or explanation may not be readily apparent and you have to figure things out. Use your common sense to interpret anything that isn't clear.

Prefixes

If you're having trouble with a word in the question or answer choices, try dissecting it. Take advantage of every clue that the word might include. Prefixes and suffixes can be a huge help. Usually they allow you to determine a basic meaning. Pre- means before, post- means after, pro - is positive, de- is negative. From these prefixes and suffixes, you can get an idea of the general meaning of the word and try to put it into context. Beware though of any traps. Just because con is the opposite of pro, doesn't necessarily mean congress is the opposite of progress!

Hedge Phrases

Watch out for critical "hedge" phrases, such as likely, may, can, will often, sometimes, often, almost, mostly, usually, generally, rarely, sometimes. Question writers insert these hedge phrases to cover every possibility. Often an answer choice will be wrong simply because it leaves no room for exception. Avoid answer choices that have definitive words like "exactly," and "always".

Switchback Words

Stay alert for "switchbacks". These are the words and phrases frequently used to alert you to shifts in thought. The most common switchback word is "but". Others include although, however, nevertheless, on the other hand, even though, while, in spite of, despite, regardless of.

New Information

Correct answer choices will rarely have completely new information included. Answer choices typically are straightforward reflections of the material asked about and will directly relate to the question. If a new piece of information is included in an answer choice that doesn't even seem to relate to the topic being asked about, then that answer choice is likely incorrect. All of the information needed to answer the question is usually provided for you, and so you should not have to make guesses that are unsupported or choose answer choices that require unknown information that cannot be reasoned on its own.

Time Management

On technical questions, don't get lost on the technical terms. Don't spend too much time on any one question. If you don't know what a term means, then since you don't have a dictionary, odds are you aren't going to get much further. You should immediately recognize terms as whether or not you know them. If you don't, work with the other clues that you have, the other answer choices and terms provided, but don't waste too much time trying to figure out a difficult term.

Contextual Clues

Look for contextual clues. An answer can be right but not correct. The contextual clues will help you find the answer that is most right and is correct. Understand the context in which a phrase or statement is made. This will help you make important distinctions.

Don't Panic

Panicking will not answer any questions for you. Therefore, it isn't helpful. When you first see the question, if your mind goes blank, take a deep breath. Force yourself to mechanically go through the steps of solving the problem and using the strategies you've learned.

Pace Yourself

Don't get clock fever. It's easy to be overwhelmed when you're looking at a page full of questions, your mind is full of random thoughts and feeling confused, and the clock is ticking down faster than you would like. Calm down and maintain the pace that you have set for yourself. As long as you are on track by monitoring your pace, you are guaranteed to have enough time for yourself. When you get to the last few minutes of the test, it may seem like you won't have enough time left, but if you only have as many questions as you should have left at that point, then you're right on track!

Answer Selection

The best way to pick an answer choice is to eliminate all of those that are wrong, until only one is left and confirm that is the correct answer. Sometimes though, an answer choice may immediately look right. Be careful! Take a second to make sure that the other choices are not equally obvious. Don't make a hasty mistake. There are only two times that you should stop before checking other answers. First is when you are positive that the answer choice you have selected is correct. Second is when time is almost out and you have to make a quick guess!

Check Your Work

Since you will probably not know every term listed and the answer to every question, it is important that you get credit for the ones that you do know. Don't miss any questions through careless mistakes. If at all possible, try to take a second to look back over your answer selection and make sure you've selected the correct answer choice and haven't made a costly careless mistake (such as marking an answer choice that you didn't mean to mark). This quick double check should more than pay for itself in caught mistakes for the time it costs.

Beware of Directly Quoted Answers

Sometimes an answer choice will repeat word for word a portion of the question or reference section. However, beware of such exact duplication – it may be a trap! More than likely, the correct choice will paraphrase or summarize a point, rather than being exactly the same wording.

Slang

Scientific sounding answers are better than slang ones. An answer choice that begins "To compare the outcomes…" is much more likely to be correct than one that begins "Because some people insisted…"

Extreme Statements

Avoid wild answers that throw out highly controversial ideas that are proclaimed as established fact. An answer choice that states the "process should be used in certain situations, if…" is much more likely to be correct than one that states the "process should be discontinued completely." The first is a calm rational statement and doesn't even make a definitive, uncompromising stance, using a hedge word "if" to provide wiggle room, whereas the second choice is a radical idea and far more extreme.

Answer Choice Families

When you have two or more answer choices that are direct opposites or parallels, one of them is usually the correct answer. For instance, if one answer choice states "x increases" and another answer choice states "x decreases" or "y increases," then those two or three answer choices are very similar in construction and fall into the same family of answer choices. A family of answer choices is when two or three answer choices are very similar in construction, and yet often have a directly opposite meaning. Usually the correct answer choice will be in that family of answer choices. The "odd man out" or answer choice that doesn't seem to fit the parallel construction of the other answer choices is more likely to be incorrect.

Special Report: How to Overcome Test Anxiety

The very nature of tests caters to some level of anxiety, nervousness or tension, just as we feel for any important event that occurs in our lives. A little bit of anxiety or nervousness can be a good thing. It helps us with motivation, and makes achievement just that much sweeter. However, too much anxiety can be a problem; especially if it hinders our ability to function and perform.

"Test anxiety," is the term that refers to the emotional reactions that some test-takers experience when faced with a test or exam. Having a fear of testing and exams is based upon a rational fear, since the test-taker's performance can shape the course of an academic career. Nevertheless, experiencing excessive fear of examinations will only interfere with the test-takers ability to perform, and his/her chances to be successful.

There are a large variety of causes that can contribute to the development and sensation of test anxiety. These include, but are not limited to lack of performance and worrying about issues surrounding the test.

Lack of Preparation

Lack of preparation can be identified by the following behaviors or situations:

Not scheduling enough time to study, and therefore cramming the night before the test or exam
Managing time poorly, to create the sensation that there is not enough time to do everything
Failing to organize the text information in advance, so that the study material consists of the entire text and not simply the pertinent information
Poor overall studying habits

Worrying, on the other hand, can be related to both the test taker, or many other factors around him/her that will be affected by the results of the test. These include worrying about:

Previous performances on similar exams, or exams in general
How friends and other students are achieving
The negative consequences that will result from a poor grade or failure

There are three primary elements to test anxiety. Physical components, which involve the same typical bodily reactions as those to acute anxiety (to be discussed below). Emotional factors have to do with fear or panic. Mental or cognitive issues concerning attention spans and memory abilities.

Physical Signals

There are many different symptoms of test anxiety, and these are not limited to mental and emotional strain. Frequently there are a range of physical signals that will let a test taker know that he/she is suffering from test anxiety. These bodily changes can include the following:

Perspiring
Sweaty palms
Wet, trembling hands
Nausea
Dry mouth
A knot in the stomach
Headache
Faintness
Muscle tension
Aching shoulders, back and neck
Rapid heart beat
Feeling too hot/cold

To recognize the sensation of test anxiety, a test-taker should monitor him/herself for the following sensations:

The physical distress symptoms as listed above
Emotional sensitivity, expressing emotional feelings such as the need to cry or laugh too much, or a sensation of anger or helplessness
A decreased ability to think, causing the test-taker to blank out or have racing thoughts that are hard to organize or control.

Though most students will feel some level of anxiety when faced with a test or exam, the majority can cope with that anxiety and maintain it at a manageable level. However, those who cannot are faced with a very real and very serious condition, which can and should be controlled for the immeasurable benefit of this sufferer.

Naturally, these sensations lead to negative results for the testing experience. The most common effects of test anxiety have to do with nervousness and mental blocking.

Nervousness

Nervousness can appear in several different levels:

The test-taker's difficulty, or even inability to read and understand the questions on the test
The difficulty or inability to organize thoughts to a coherent form
The difficulty or inability to recall key words and concepts relating to the testing questions (especially essays)
The receipt of poor grades on a test, though the test material was well known by the test taker

Conversely, a person may also experience mental blocking, which involves:

Blanking out on test questions
Only remembering the correct answers to the questions when the test has already finished.

Fortunately for test anxiety sufferers, beating these feelings, to a large degree, has to do with proper preparation. When a test taker has a feeling of preparedness, then anxiety will be dramatically lessened.

The first step to resolving anxiety issues is to distinguish which of the two types of anxiety are being suffered. If the anxiety is a direct result of a lack of preparation, this should be considered a normal reaction, and the anxiety level (as opposed to the test results) shouldn't be anything to worry about. However, if, when adequately prepared, the test-taker still panics, blanks out, or seems to overreact, this is not a fully rational reaction. While this can be considered normal too, there are many ways to combat and overcome these effects.

Remember that anxiety cannot be entirely eliminated, however, there are ways to minimize it, to make the anxiety easier to manage. Preparation is one of the best ways to minimize test anxiety. Therefore the following techniques are wise in order to best fight off any anxiety that may want to build.

To begin with, try to avoid cramming before a test, whenever it is possible. By trying to memorize an entire term's worth of information in one day, you'll be shocking your system, and not giving yourself a very good chance to absorb the information. This is an easy path to anxiety, so for those who suffer from test anxiety, cramming should not even be considered an option.

Instead of cramming, work throughout the semester to combine all of the material which is presented throughout the semester, and work on it gradually as the course goes by, making sure to master the main concepts first, leaving minor details for a week or so before the test.

To study for the upcoming exam, be sure to pose questions that may be on the examination, to gauge the ability to answer them by integrating the ideas from your texts, notes and lectures, as well as any supplementary readings.

If it is truly impossible to cover all of the information that was covered in that particular term, concentrate on the most important portions, that can be covered very well. Learn these concepts as best as possible, so that when the test comes, a goal can be made to use these concepts as presentations of your knowledge.

In addition to study habits, changes in attitude are critical to beating a struggle with test anxiety. In fact, an improvement of the perspective over the entire test-taking experience can actually help a test taker to enjoy studying and therefore improve the overall experience. Be certain not to overemphasize the significance of the grade - know that the result of the test is neither a reflection of self worth, nor is it a measure of intelligence; one grade will not predict a person's future success.

To improve an overall testing outlook, the following steps should be tried:

Keeping in mind that the most reasonable expectation for taking a test is to expect to try to demonstrate as much of what you know as you possibly can. Reminding ourselves that a test is only one test; this is not the only one, and there will be others.

The thought of thinking of oneself in an irrational, all-or-nothing term should be avoided at all costs.

A reward should be designated for after the test, so there's something to look forward to. Whether it be going to a movie, going out to eat, or simply visiting friends, schedule it in advance, and do it no matter what result is expected on the exam.

Test-takers should also keep in mind that the basics are some of the most important things, even beyond anti-anxiety techniques and studying. Never neglect the basic social, emotional and biological needs, in order to try to absorb information. In order to best achieve, these three factors must be held as just as important as the studying itself.

Study Steps

Remember the following important steps for studying:

Maintain healthy nutrition and exercise habits. Continue both your recreational activities and social pass times. These both contribute to your physical and emotional well being.

Be certain to get a good amount of sleep, especially the night before the test, because when you're overtired you are not able to perform to the best of your best ability.

Keep the studying pace to a moderate level by taking breaks when they are needed, and varying the work whenever possible, to keep the mind fresh instead of getting bored.

When enough studying has been done that all the material that can be learned has been learned, and the test taker is prepared for the test, stop studying and do something relaxing such as listening to music, watching a movie, or taking a warm bubble bath.

There are also many other techniques to minimize the uneasiness or apprehension that is experienced along with test anxiety before, during, or even after the examination. In fact, there are a great deal of things that can be done to stop anxiety from interfering with lifestyle and performance. Again, remember that anxiety will not be eliminated entirely, and it shouldn't be. Otherwise that "up" feeling for exams would not exist, and most of us depend on that sensation to perform better than usual. However, this anxiety has to be at a level that is manageable.

Of course, as we have just discussed, being prepared for the exam is half the battle right away. Attending all classes, finding out what knowledge will be expected on the exam, and knowing the exam schedules are easy steps to lowering anxiety. Keeping up with work will remove the need to cram, and efficient study habits will eliminate wasted time. Studying should be done in an ideal location for concentration, so that it is simple to become interested in the material and give it complete attention. A method such as SQ3R (Survey, Question, Read, Recite, Review) is a wonderful key to follow to make sure that the study habits are as effective as possible, especially in the case of learning from a textbook. Flashcards are great techniques for memorization. Learning to take good notes will mean that notes will be full of useful information, so that less sifting will need to be done to seek out what is pertinent for studying. Reviewing notes after class and then again on occasion will keep the information fresh in the mind. From notes that have been taken summary sheets and outlines can be made for simpler reviewing.

A study group can also be a very motivational and helpful place to study, as there will be a sharing of ideas, all of the minds can work together, to make sure that everyone understands, and the studying will be made more interesting because it will be a social occasion.

Basically, though, as long as the test-taker remains organized and self confident, with efficient study habits, less time will need to be spent studying, and higher grades will be achieved.

To become self confident, there are many useful steps. The first of these is "self talk." It has been shown through extensive research, that self-talk for students who suffer from test anxiety, should be well monitored, in order to make sure that it contributes to self confidence as opposed to sinking the student. Frequently the self talk of test-anxious students is negative or self-defeating, thinking that everyone else is smarter and faster, that they always mess up, and that if they don't do well, they'll fail the entire course. It is important to decreasing anxiety that awareness is made of self talk. Try writing any negative self thoughts and then disputing them with a positive statement instead. Begin self-encouragement as though it was a friend speaking. Repeat positive statements to help reprogram the mind to believing in successes instead of failures.

Helpful Techniques

Other extremely helpful techniques include:

Self-visualization of doing well and reaching goals
While aiming for an "A" level of understanding, don't try to "overprotect" by setting your expectations lower. This will only convince the mind to stop studying in order to meet the lower expectations.
Don't make comparisons with the results or habits of other students. These are individual factors, and different things work for different people, causing different results.
Strive to become an expert in learning what works well, and what can be done in order to improve. Consider collecting this data in a journal.
Create rewards for after studying instead of doing things before studying that will only turn into avoidance behaviors.
Make a practice of relaxing - by using methods such as progressive relaxation, self-hypnosis, guided imagery, etc - in order to make relaxation an automatic sensation.
Work on creating a state of relaxed concentration so that concentrating will take on the focus of the mind, so that none will be wasted on worrying.
Take good care of the physical self by eating well and getting enough sleep.
Plan in time for exercise and stick to this plan.

Beyond these techniques, there are other methods to be used before, during and after the test that will help the test-taker perform well in addition to overcoming anxiety.

Before the exam comes the academic preparation. This involves establishing a study schedule and beginning at least one week before the actual date of the test. By doing this, the anxiety of not having enough time to study for the test will be automatically eliminated. Moreover, this will make the studying a much more effective experience, ensuring that the learning will be an easier process. This relieves much undue pressure on the test-taker.

Summary sheets, note cards, and flash cards with the main concepts and examples of these main concepts should be prepared in advance of the actual studying time. A topic should never be eliminated from this process. By omitting a topic because it isn't expected to be on the test is only setting up the test-taker for anxiety should it actually appear on the exam. Utilize the course syllabus for laying out the topics that should be studied. Carefully go over the notes that were made in class, paying special attention to any of the issues that the professor took special care to emphasize while lecturing in class. In the textbooks, use the chapter review, or if possible, the chapter tests, to begin your review.

It may even be possible to ask the instructor what information will be covered on the exam, or what the format of the exam will be (for example, multiple choice, essay, free form, true-false). Additionally, see if it is possible to find out how many questions will be on the test. If a review sheet or sample test has been offered by the professor, make good use of it, above anything else, for the preparation for the test. Another great resource for getting to know the examination is reviewing tests from previous semesters. Use these tests to review, and aim to achieve a 100% score on each of the possible topics. With a few exceptions, the goal that you set for yourself is the highest one that you will reach.

Take all of the questions that were assigned as homework, and rework them to any other possible course material. The more problems reworked, the more skill and confidence will form as a result. When forming the solution to a problem, write out each of the steps. Don't simply do head work. By doing as many steps on paper as possible, much clarification and therefore confidence will be formed. Do this with as many homework problems as possible, before checking the answers. By checking the answer after each problem, a reinforcement will exist, that will not be on the exam. Study situations should be as exam-like as possible, to prime the test-taker's system for the experience. By waiting to check the answers at the end, a psychological advantage will be formed, to decrease the stress factor.

Another fantastic reason for not cramming is the avoidance of confusion in concepts, especially when it comes to mathematics. 8-10 hours of study will become one hundred percent more effective if it is spread out over a week or at least several days, instead of doing it all in one sitting. Recognize that the human brain requires time in order to assimilate new material, so frequent breaks and a span of study time over several days will be much more beneficial.

Additionally, don't study right up until the point of the exam. Studying should stop a minimum of one hour before the exam begins. This allows the brain to rest and put things in their proper order. This will also provide the time to become as relaxed as possible when going into the examination room. The test-taker will also have time to eat well and eat sensibly. Know that the brain needs food as much as the rest of the body. With enough food and enough sleep, as well as a relaxed attitude, the body and the mind are primed for success.

Avoid any anxious classmates who are talking about the exam. These students only spread anxiety, and are not worth sharing the anxious sentimentalities.

Before the test also involves creating a positive attitude, so mental preparation should also be a point of concentration. There are many keys to creating a positive attitude. Should fears become rushing in, make a visualization of taking the exam, doing well, and seeing an A written on the paper. Write out a list of affirmations that will bring a feeling of confidence, such as "I am doing well in my English class," "I studied well and know my material," "I enjoy this class." Even if the affirmations aren't believed at first, it sends a positive message to the subconscious which will result in an alteration of the overall belief system, which is the system that creates reality.

If a sensation of panic begins, work with the fear and imagine the very worst! Work through the entire scenario of not passing the test, failing the entire course, and dropping out of school, followed by not getting a job, and pushing a shopping cart through the dark alley where you'll live. This will place things into perspective! Then, practice deep breathing and create a visualization of the opposite situation - achieving an "A" on the exam, passing the entire course, receiving the degree at a graduation ceremony.

On the day of the test, there are many things to be done to ensure the best results, as well as the most calm outlook. The following stages are suggested in order to maximize test-taking potential:

Begin the examination day with a moderate breakfast, and avoid any coffee or beverages with caffeine if the test taker is prone to jitters. Even people who are used to managing caffeine can feel jittery or light-headed when it is taken on a test day.
Attempt to do something that is relaxing before the examination begins. As last minute cramming clouds the mastering of overall concepts, it is better to use this time to create a calming outlook.
Be certain to arrive at the test location well in advance, in order to provide time to select a location that is away from doors, windows and other distractions, as well as giving enough time to relax before the test begins.
Keep away from anxiety generating classmates who will upset the sensation of stability and relaxation that is being attempted before the exam.
Should the waiting period before the exam begins cause anxiety, create a self-distraction by reading a light magazine or something else that is relaxing and simple.

During the exam itself, read the entire exam from beginning to end, and find out how much time should be allotted to each individual problem. Once writing the exam, should more time be taken for a problem, it should be abandoned, in order to begin another problem. If there is time at the end, the unfinished problem can always be returned to and completed.

Read the instructions very carefully - twice - so that unpleasant surprises won't follow during or after the exam has ended.

When writing the exam, pretend that the situation is actually simply the completion of homework within a library, or at home. This will assist in forming a relaxed atmosphere, and will allow the brain extra focus for the complex thinking function.

Begin the exam with all of the questions with which the most confidence is felt. This will build the confidence level regarding the entire exam and will begin a quality momentum. This will also create encouragement for trying the problems where uncertainty resides.

Going with the "gut instinct" is always the way to go when solving a problem. Second guessing should be avoided at all costs. Have confidence in the ability to do well.

For essay questions, create an outline in advance that will keep the mind organized and make certain that all of the points are remembered. For multiple choice, read every answer, even if the correct one has been spotted - a better one may exist.

Continue at a pace that is reasonable and not rushed, in order to be able to work carefully. Provide enough time to go over the answers at the end, to check for small errors that can be corrected.

Should a feeling of panic begin, breathe deeply, and think of the feeling of the body releasing sand through its pores. Visualize a calm, peaceful place, and include all of the sights, sounds and sensations of this image. Continue the deep breathing, and take a few minutes to continue this with closed eyes. When all is well again, return to the test.

If a "blanking" occurs for a certain question, skip it and move on to the next question. There will be time to return to the other question later. Get everything done that can be done, first, to guarantee all the grades that can be compiled, and to build all of the confidence possible. Then return to the weaker questions to build the marks from there.

Remember, one's own reality can be created, so as long as the belief is there, success will follow. And remember: anxiety can happen later, right now, there's an exam to be written!

After the examination is complete, whether there is a feeling for a good grade or a bad grade, don't dwell on the exam, and be certain to follow through on the reward that was promised...and enjoy it! Don't dwell on any mistakes that have been made, as there is nothing that can be done at this point anyway.

Additionally, don't begin to study for the next test right away. Do something relaxing for a while, and let the mind relax and prepare itself to begin absorbing information again.

From the results of the exam - both the grade and the entire experience, be certain to learn from what has gone on. Perfect studying habits and work some more on confidence in order to make the next examination experience even better than the last one.

Learn to avoid places where openings occurred for laziness, procrastination and day dreaming.

Use the time between this exam and the next one to better learn to relax, even learning to relax on cue, so that any anxiety can be controlled during the next exam. Learn how to relax the body. Slouch in your chair if that helps. Tighten and then relax all of the different muscle groups, one group at a time, beginning with the feet and then working all the way up to the neck and face. This will ultimately relax the muscles more than they were to begin with. Learn how to breathe deeply and comfortably, and focus on this breathing going in and out as a relaxing thought. With every exhale, repeat the word "relax."

As common as test anxiety is, it is very possible to overcome it. Make yourself one of the test-takers who overcome this frustrating hindrance.

Special Report: Additional Bonus Material

Due to our efforts to try to keep this book to a manageable length, we've created a link that will give you access to all of your additional bonus material.

Please visit http://www.mometrix.com/bonus948/poss to access the information.